BOOK 3

English No Problem!

Jenni Currie Santamaría
ABC Adult School
Los Angeles Unified School District
Cerritos, CA

Mary Myers-Hall
ABC Adult School
Los Angeles Unified School District
Cerritos, CA

New Readers Press

English—No Problem!®
English—No Problem! Level 3 Student Book
ISBN 978-1-56420-358-8

Copyright © 2004 New Readers Press
New Readers Press
ProLiteracy's Publishing Division
104 Marcellus Street, Syracuse, New York 13204
www.newreaderspress.com

Printed in the United States of America
10

Proceeds from the sale of New Readers Press materials support professional development, training, and technical assistance programs of ProLiteracy that benefit local literacy programs in the U.S. and around the globe.

Acquisitions Editor: Paula L. Schlusberg
Developer: Mendoza and Associates
Project Director: Roseanne Mendoza
Project Editor: Pat Harrington-Wydell
Content Editor: Judi Lauber
Production Director: Heather Witt-Badoud
Designer: Kimbrly Koennecke
Illustrations: Linda Tiff, James Wallace
Production Specialist: Alexander Jones
Cover Design: Kimbrly Koennecke
Cover Photography: Robert Mescavage Photography
Photo Credits: Hal Silverman Studio

Authors

Jenni Currie Santamaría
ABC Adult School
Los Angeles Unified School District
Cerritos, CA

Mary Myers-Hall
ABC Adult School
Los Angeles Unified School District
Cerritos, CA

Contributors

National Council Members
Audrey Abed, *San Marcos Even Start Program, San Marcos, TX*
Myra K. Baum, *New York City Board of Education (retired), New York, NY*
Kathryn Hamilton, *Elk Grove Adult and Community Education, Sacramento, CA*
Brigitte Marshall, *Oakland Adult Education Programs, Oakland, CA*
Teri McLean, *Florida Human Resources Development Center, Gainesville, FL*
Alan Seaman, *Wheaton College, Wheaton, IL*

Reviewers
Sabrina Budasi-Martin, *William Rainey Harper College, Palatine, IL*
Linda Davis-Pluta, *Oakton Community College, Des Plaines, IL*
Patricia DeHesus-Lopez, *Center for Continuing Education, Texas A&M University, Kingsville, TX*
Gail Feinstein Forman, *San Diego City College, San Diego, CA*
Carolyn Harding, *Marshall High School Adult Program, Falls Church, VA*
Trish Kerns, *Old Marshall Adult Education Center, Sacramento City Unified School District, Sacramento, CA*
Lydia Omori, *William Rainey Harper College, Palatine, IL*
Debe Pack-Garcia, *Manteca Adult School, Humbolt, CA*
Pamela Patterson, *Seminole Community College, Sanford, FL*
Catherine Porter, *Adult Learning Resource Center, Des Plaines, IL*
Jean Rose, *ABC Adult School, Cerritos, CA*
Eric Rosenbaum, *Bronx Community College Adult Program, Bronx, NY*
Laurie Shapero, *Miami-Dade Community College, Miami, FL*
Terry Shearer, *North Harris College Community Education, Houston, TX*
Abigail Tom, *Durham Technical Community College, Chapel Hill, NC*
Darla Wickard, *North Harris College Community Education, Houston, TX*

Pilot Teachers
Connie Bateman, *Gerber Adult Education Center, Sacramento, CA*
Jennifer Bell, *William Rainey Harper College, Palatine, IL*
Marguerite Bock, *Chula Vista Adult School, Chula Vista, CA*
Giza Braun, *National City Adult School, National City, CA*
Sabrina Budasi-Martin, *William Rainey Harper College, Palatine, IL*
Wong-Ling Chew, *Citizens Advice Bureau, Bronx, NY*
Renee Collins, *Elk Grove Adult and Community Education, Sacramento, CA*
Rosette Dawson, *North Harris College Community Education, Houston, TX*
Kathleen Edel, *Elk Grove Adult and Community Education, Sacramento, CA*
Margaret Erwin, *Elk Grove Adult and Community Education, Sacramento, CA*
Teresa L. Gonzalez, *North Harris College Community Education, Houston, TX*
Fernando L. Herbert, *Bronx Adult School, Bronx, NY*
Carolyn Killean, *North Harris College Community Education, Houston, TX*

Elizabeth Minicz, *William Rainey Harper College, Palatine, IL*
Larry Moore, *Long Beach Adult School, Long Beach, CA*
Lydia Omori, *William Rainey Harper College, Palatine, IL*
Valsa Panikulam, *William Rainey Harper College, Palatine, IL*
Kathryn Powell, *William Rainey Harper College, Palatine, IL*
Alan Reiff, *NYC Board of Education, Adult and Continuing Education, Bronx, NY*
Brenda M. Rodriguez, *San Marcos Even Start, San Marcos, TX*
Juan Carlos Rodriguez, *San Marcos Even Start, San Marcos, TX*
Joan Siff, *NYC Board of Education, Adult and Continuing Education, Bronx, NY*
Susie Simon, *Long Beach Adult School, Long Beach, CA*
Gina Tauber, *North Harris College, Houston, TX*
Diane Villanueva, *Elk Grove Adult and Community Education, Sacramento, CA*
Dona Wayment, *Elk Grove Adult and Community Education, Sacramento, CA*
Weihua Wen, *NYC Board of Education, Adult and Continuing Education, Bronx, NY*
Darla Wickard, *North Harris College Community Education, Houston, TX*
Judy Wurtz, *Sweetwater Union High School District, Chula Vista, CA*

Focus Group Participants
Leslie Jo Adams, *Laguna Niguel, CA*
Fiona Armstrong, *New York City Board of Education, New York, NY*
Myra K. Baum, *New York City Board of Education (retired), New York, NY*
Gretchen Bitterlin, *San Diego Unified School District, San Diego, CA*
Diana Della Costa, *Worksite ESOL Programs, Kissimmee, FL*
Patricia DeHesus-Lopez, *Center for Continuing Education, Texas A&M University, Kingsville, TX*
Frankie Dovel, *Orange County Public Schools, VESOL Program, Orlando, FL*
Marianne Dryden, *Region 1 Education Service Center, Edinburgh, TX*
Richard Firsten, *Lindsay Hopkins Technical Center, Miami, FL*
Pamela S. Forbes, *Bartlett High School, Elgin, IL*
Kathryn Hamilton, *Elk Grove Adult and Community Education, Sacramento, CA*
Trish Kerns, *Old Marshall Adult Education Center, Sacramento City Unified School District, Sacramento, CA*
Suzanne Leibman, *The College of Lake County, Grayslake, IL*
Patti Long, *Old Marshall Adult Education Center, Sacramento City Unified School District, Sacramento, CA*
Brigitte Marshall, *Oakland Adult Education Programs, Oakland, CA*
Bet Messmer, *Santa Clara Adult School, Santa Clara, CA*
Patricia Mooney, *New York State Board of Education, Albany, NY*
Lee Ann Moore, *Salinas Adult School, Salinas, CA*
Lynne Nicodemus, *San Juan Adult School, Carmichael, CA*
Pamela Patterson, *Seminole Community College, Sanford, FL*
Eric Rosenbaum, *Bronx Community College, Bronx, NY*
Federico Salas, *North Harris College Community Education, Houston, TX*
Linda Sasser, *Alhambra District Office, Alhambra, CA*
Alan Seaman, *Wheaton College, Wheaton, IL*
Kathleen Slattery, *Salinas Adult School, Salinas, CA*
Carol Speigl, *Center for Continuing Education, Texas A&M University, Kingsville, TX*
Edie Uber, *Santa Clara Adult School, Santa Clara, CA*
Lise Wanage, *CASAS, Phoenix, AZ*

About This Series

Meeting Adult Learners' Needs with *English—No Problem!*

English—No Problem! is a theme-based, performance-based series focused on developing critical thinking and cultural awareness and on building language and life skills. Designed for adult and young adult English language learners, the series addresses themes and issues meaningful to adults in the United States.

English—No Problem! is appropriate for and respectful of adult learners. These are some key features:
- interactive, communicative, participatory approach
- rich, authentic language
- problem-posing methodology
- project-based units and task-based lessons
- goal setting embedded in each unit and lesson
- units organized around themes of adult relevance
- contextualized, inductive grammar
- student materials designed to fit into lesson plans
- performance assessment, including tools for learner self-evaluation

Series Themes

Across the series, units have the following themes:
- Life Stages: Personal Growth and Goal Setting
- Making Connections
- Taking Care of Yourself
- Personal Finance
- Consumer Awareness
- Protecting Your Legal Rights
- Participating in Your New Country and Community
- Lifelong Learning
- Celebrating Success

At each level, these themes are narrowed to subthemes that are level-appropriate in content and language.

English—No Problem! Series Components

Five levels make up the series:
- literacy
- level 1 (low beginning)
- level 2 (high beginning)
- level 3 (low intermediate)
- level 4 (high intermediate)

The series includes the following components.

Student Book

A full-color student book is the core of each level of *English—No Problem!* Literacy skills, vocabulary, grammar, reading, writing, listening, speaking, and SCANS-type skills are taught and practiced.

Teacher's Edition

Each teacher's edition includes these tools:
- general suggestions for using the series
- scope and sequence charts for the level
- lesson-specific teacher notes with reduced student book pages
- complete scripts for all listening activities and Pronunciation Targets in the student book

Workbook

A workbook provides contextualized practice in the skills taught at each level. Activities relate to the student book stories. Workbook activities are especially useful for learners working individually.

 This icon in the teacher's edition indicates where workbook activities can be assigned.

Reproducible Masters

The reproducible masters include photocopiable materials for the level. Some masters are unit-specific, such as contextualized vocabulary and grammar activities, games, and activities focusing on higher-level thinking skills. Others are generic graphic organizers. Still other masters can be used by teachers, peers, and learners themselves to assess the work done in each unit.

Each masters book also includes scripts for all listening activities in the masters. (Note: These activities are *not* included on the *English—No Problem!* audio recordings.)

 This icon in the teacher's edition indicates where reproducible masters can be used.

Audio Recording

Available on CD and cassette, each level's audio component includes listening passages, listening activities, and Pronunciation Targets from the student book.

 This icon in the student book and teacher's edition indicates that the audio recording includes material for that activity.

Lesson-Plan Builder

This free, web-based *Lesson-Plan Builder* allows teachers to create and save customized lesson plans, related graphic organizers, and selected assessment masters. Goals, vocabulary lists, and other elements are already in the template for each lesson. Teachers then add their own notes to customize their plans. They can also create original graphic organizers using generic templates.

When a lesson plan is finished, the customized materials can be printed and stored in PDF form.

This icon in the teacher's edition refers teachers to the *Lesson-Plan Builder,* found at www.enp.newreaderspress.com.

Vocabulary Cards

For literacy, level 1, and level 2, all vocabulary from the Picture Dictionaries and Vocabulary boxes in the student books is also presented on reproducible flash cards. At the literacy level, the cards also include capital letters, lowercase letters, and numerals.

Placement Tool

The Placement Test student booklet includes items that measure exit skills for each level of the series so that learners can start work in the appropriate student book. The teacher's guide includes a listening script, as well as guidelines for administering the test to a group, for giving an optional oral test, and for interpreting scores.

Hot Topics in ESL

These online professional development articles by adult ESL experts focus on key issues and instructional techniques embodied in *English—No Problem!,* providing background information to enhance effective use of the materials. They are available online at www.enp.newreaderspress.com.

Addressing the Standards

English—No Problem! has been correlated from the earliest stages of development with national standards for adult education and ESL, including the NRS (National Reporting System), EFF (Equipped for the Future), SCANS (Secretary's Commission on Achieving Necessary Skills), CASAS (Comprehensive Adult Student Assessment System) competencies, BEST (Basic English Skills Test), and SPLs (Student Performance Levels). The series also reflects state standards from New York, California, and Florida.

About the Student Books

Each unit in the student books includes a two-page unit opener followed by three lessons (two at the literacy level). A cumulative unit project concludes each unit. Every unit addresses all four language skills—

listening, speaking, reading, and writing. Each lesson focuses on characters operating in one of the three EFF-defined adult roles—parent/family member at home, worker at school or work, or citizen/community member in the larger community.

Unit Opener Pages

Unit Goals The vocabulary, language, pronunciation, and culture goals set forth in the unit opener correlate to a variety of state and national standards.

Opening Question and Photo The opening question, photo, and caption introduce the unit protagonists and engage learners affectively in issues the unit explores.

Think and Talk This feature of levels 1–4 presents questions based on classic steps in problem-posing methodology, adjusted and simplified as needed.

What's Your Opinion? In levels 1–4, this deliberately controversial question often appears after Think and Talk or on the first page of a lesson. It is designed to encourage lively teacher-directed discussion, even among learners with limited vocabulary.

Picture Dictionary or Vocabulary Box This feature introduces important unit vocabulary and concepts.

Gather Your Thoughts In levels 1–4, this activity helps learners relate the unit theme to their own lives. They record their thoughts in a graphic organizer, following a model provided.

What's the Problem? This activity, which follows Gather Your Thoughts, encourages learners to practice another step in problem posing. They identify a possible problem and apply the issue to their own lives.

Setting Goals This feature of levels 1–4 is the first step of a unit's self-evaluation strand. Learners choose from a list of language and life goals and add their own goal to the list. The goals are related to the lesson activities and tasks and to the unit project. After completing a unit, learners revisit these goals in Check Your Progress, the last page of each workbook unit.

First Lesson Page

While the unit opener sets up an issue or problem, the lessons involve learners in seeking solutions while simultaneously developing language competencies.

Lesson Goals and EFF Role The lesson opener lists language, culture, and life-skill goals and identifies the EFF role depicted in that lesson.

Pre-Reading or Pre-Listening Question This question prepares learners to seek solutions to the issues presented in the reading or listening passage or lesson graphic that follows.

Reading or Listening Tip At levels 1–4, this feature presents comprehension and analysis strategies used by good listeners and readers.

Lesson Stimulus Each lesson starts with a reading passage (a picture story at the literacy level), a listening passage, or a lesson graphic. A photo on the page sets the situation for a listening passage. Each listening passage is included in the audio recording, and scripts are provided at the end of the student book and the teacher's edition. A lesson graphic may be a schedule, chart, diagram, graph, time line, or similar item. The questions that follow each lesson stimulus focus on comprehension and analysis.

Remaining Lesson Pages

Picture Dictionary, Vocabulary Box, and Idiom Watch These features present the active lesson vocabulary. At lower levels, pictures often help convey meaning. Vocabulary boxes for the literacy level also include letters and numbers. At levels 3 and 4, idioms are included in every unit.

Class, Group, or Partner Chat This interactive feature provides a model miniconversation. The model sets up a real-life exchange that encourages use of the lesson vocabulary and grammatical structures. Learners ask highly structured and controlled questions and record classmates' responses in a graphic organizer.

Grammar Talk At levels 1–4, the target grammatical structure is presented in several examples. Following the examples is a short explanation or question that guides learners to come up with a rule on their own. At the literacy level, language boxes highlight basic grammatical structures without formal teaching.

Pronunciation Target In this feature of levels 1–4, learners answer questions that lead them to discover pronunciation rules for themselves.

Chat Follow-Ups Learners use information they recorded during the Chat activity. They write patterned sentences, using lesson vocabulary and structures.

In the US This feature is a short cultural reading or brief explanation of some aspect of US culture.

Compare Cultures At levels 1–4, this follow-up to In the US asks learners to compare the custom or situation in the US to similar ones in their home countries.

Activities A, B, C, etc. These practice activities, most of them interactive, apply what has been learned in the lesson so far.

Lesson Tasks Each lesson concludes with a task that encourages learners to apply the skills taught and practiced earlier. Many tasks involve pair or group work, as well as follow-up presentations to the class.

Challenge Reading

At level 4, a two-page reading follows the lessons. This feature helps learners develop skills that prepare them for longer readings they will encounter in future study or higher-level jobs.

Unit Project

Each unit concludes with a final project in which learners apply all or many of the skills they acquired in the unit. The project consists of carefully structured and sequenced individual, pair, and group activities. These projects also help develop important higher-level skills such as planning, organizing, collaborating, and presenting.

Additional Features

The following minifeatures appear as needed at different levels:

One Step Up These extensions of an activity, task, or unit project allow learners to work at a slightly higher skill level. This feature is especially useful when classes include learners at multiple levels.

Attention Boxes These unlabeled boxes highlight words and structures that are not taught explicitly in the lesson, but that learners may need. Teachers are encouraged to point out these words and structures and to offer any explanations that learners require.

Remember? These boxes present, in abbreviated form, previously introduced vocabulary and language structures.

Writing Extension This feature encourages learners to do additional writing. It is usually a practical rather than an academic activity.

Technology Extra This extension gives learners guidelines for doing part of an activity, task, or project using such technology as computers, photocopiers, and audio and video recorders.

Contents

Closing the Gap

◆ **Vocabulary** Words that describe people and activities
◆ **Language** Present-tense questions and statements
  • Compound sentences
◆ **Pronunciation** Contrasting sounds • Linking
◆ **Culture** Women in sports

What kinds of things do people of different ages like to do?

Mina lives with her father, who is from India, and her teenage daughter, Annie. Mina's mother died two years ago, and her father is lonely. He wants Mina and Annie to spend more time with him. Mina thinks that her father needs new interests.

Think and Talk

1. What do you see in the photograph?
2. What kinds of things do you think Mina, Annie, and Mina's father are interested in?
3. Could their different interests cause conflict among them? Explain.
4. Do the people in your family have different interests? Explain.

What's Your Opinion? Many young people in the US are very active in after-school activities and sports. This means that they spend many afternoons away from home. Do you think that this is OK? Describe a situation when this might be OK and one when it's not OK.

Gather Your Thoughts Think about people who you know and the things that they like to do. Categorize them in an idea map like the one below.

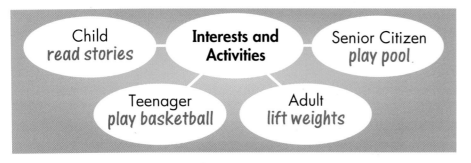

Child
read stories

Interests and Activities

Senior Citizen
play pool

Teenager
play basketball

Adult
lift weights

In your group, compare your idea maps. See if people from the same age group have similar interests.

With your class, write sentences that connect ideas from your idea map with the vocabulary words. Write the sentences on the board.

Mina feels confident when she lifts weights.

What's the Problem? People of different ages have different interests. What kinds of things stop people from doing what they like to do? How are the problems different for people of different ages? Think or talk with a partner.

Setting Goals The skills below will help you and your family learn about different kinds of opportunities in your community. Which goals are most important to you? Rank them from 1 (most important) to 6.

_____ **a.** ask for information over the phone

_____ **b.** express agreement and disagreement

_____ **c.** talk to people about my interests

_____ **d.** understand phone recordings

_____ **e.** explain how to do an activity

_____ **f.** another goal: _____

Which was the most important goal for your class? Tally your answers. Talk about your most important goals.

Vocabulary

Repeat these words after your teacher. Talk about their meanings. Write the words in your notebook. With a partner, write a sentence using each word.

confidence/confident

conflict

fulfill

generation

join

opportunity

participate

Idiom Watch!
close the gap

Activities for Young and Old

- Learn how to get information about local activities
- Use present-tense questions and statements

Do you take classes just for fun? What kinds? Where?

lectures

options

special interest

- **Listening Tip** 🎧 Focusing on specific information can help you understand what you hear. This recording lists the classes at the community center. Read the questions below, and then listen for specific information. Close your book and listen to your teacher or the audio. You can read the words on page 118.

Mina is calling the community center to get more information about activities for seniors. Since her mother died, her father has been alone at home during the day. She knows that a few men from India go to the center, and she thinks that her father would enjoy it.

Talk or Write   Listen to the recording again. Then answer the questions.
1. Which number do you press for information about teen basketball?
2. What age group can participate in senior activities?
3. How many days a week is the community center open?
4. What does Mina ask for? Why does she spell her last name?

Group Chat Talk to your group about activities that you like and don't like. Ask each other these questions. Take notes in a chart like this one.

What's your name?	What do you like?	What don't you like?
Sonya	swimming	cheerleading

Vocabulary

Repeat these words after your teacher. Talk about their meanings. Write the words in your notebook. With a partner, write a sentence using each word.

- aerobics
- ceramics
- cheerleading
- chess
- crafts
- gymnastics
- lectures
- martial arts

Grammar Talk: Present-Tense Questions and Statements

Is the Senior Center open on Sundays?	The Senior Center **isn't** open on Sundays.
Does the Senior Center **offer** aerobics?	The Senior Center **offers** aerobics.
When **does** the Senior Center **open**?	The Senior Center **opens** at 7:30 A.M.
Where **do** we **go** for lectures?	We **go** to room 23 for lectures.

Which questions have do *or* does? *Why? Which statements have verbs that end in* s? *Why do they end in* s? *With your class, write rules for present-tense questions and answers with* be *and with other verbs.*

Pronunciation Target • Linking

🎧 *Listen to your teacher or the audio.*

What time does the par<u>k o</u>pen?
When does this clas<u>s e</u>nd?

Do you ha<u>ve a</u>ctivities for seniors?
The center offer<u>s a</u>erobics.

A consonant sound at the end of a word links, *or connects, to the beginning vowel of the next word. Practice linking the underlined sounds from the sentences above.*

Activity A 🎧 Listen to your teacher or the audio. Write the sentences that you hear. Listen again and check your writing for correct punctuation. Can you find the linking sounds? Underline the linking sounds. Practice the sounds by reading the sentences to your partner.

Activity B **Group Chat Follow-Up** Look at the chart from your Group Chat on page 13. In your notebook, write sentences about your group members.

Sonya likes swimming. She doesn't like cheerleading.

Activity C 🎧 Listen to your teacher or the audio. You will hear questions about activities. Listen again and fill in the missing words.

1. Do you _____ that aerobics is fun?

2. _____ the community college offer aquatics?

3. _____ cheerleading popular in your home country?

4. _____ do people make in a ceramics class?

5. Do you _____ how to play chess?

6. Do you like to _____ crafts?

7. What kinds of lectures _____ interesting to you?

8. _____ can children learn gymnastics?

9. _____ many people practice martial arts in your home country?

Correct your answers with your class. When you finish, ask your partner the questions.

 TASK 1: Role-Play a Phone Conversation

In pairs, choose an activity that you are interested in. Write questions to ask an organization that offers the activity. Leave space between the questions to write the answers.

Role-play a phone call with your partner. Your partner should answer the phone with the name of the place you are calling. You can say

- "I'm calling for information about _____."
- "I'd like some information about _____."
- "I'd like to know about _____."

Ask your partner the questions you wrote. When your partner gives you an answer, repeat the information before you write it down.
You can end your conversation like this: "Thank you for your help."

One Step Up

a. Role-play a phone call to one of your friends. Ask if your friend would like to go to a class with you.

b. Call a community organization and ask questions about activities that they offer. Report back to the class.

Conflict at the Office

◆ Express agreement and disagreement
◆ Use compound sentences

Do you know anyone who has had a conflict at work with someone of a different age? What happened? Why did it happen?

casual

dress code

enhance

impression

judgment

◆ **Reading Tip** Words in large type can give you information about what you will find in a reading. Read the words in large type on this web site. What advice do you think it will give? Read to see if you were correct.

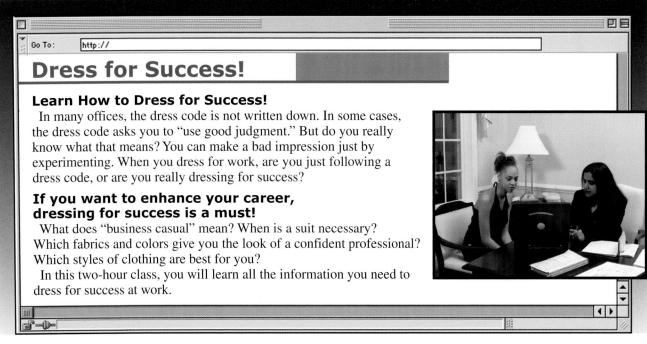

Go To: http://

Dress for Success!

Learn How to Dress for Success!
  In many offices, the dress code is not written down. In some cases, the dress code asks you to "use good judgment." But do you really know what that means? You can make a bad impression just by experimenting. When you dress for work, are you just following a dress code, or are you really dressing for success?

If you want to enhance your career, dressing for success is a must!
  What does "business casual" mean? When is a suit necessary? Which fabrics and colors give you the look of a confident professional? Which styles of clothing are best for you?
  In this two-hour class, you will learn all the information you need to dress for success at work.

Mina is an office manager. She is showing a "Dress for Success" web site to an office worker named Trish.

Talk or Write
1. Why do you think Mina is showing the web site to Trish?
2. Do you think that Trish is interested in the class? Explain.

What's Your Opinion? The "Dress for Success" class is for people who work in offices. Think about other kinds of jobs. What do people usually wear? Do you think the way people dress at work is important? Do you think that people of different ages feel differently about this?

Class Chat Brainstorm opinions that might cause conflict between generations at work or school. Write them on the board.

Work with a partner. One person is A and the other is B. Use statements from the board to complete a chart like the one below.

Vocabulary

Repeat these words after your teacher. Talk about their meanings. Write the words in your notebook. With a partner, write a sentence using each word.

flexible/inflexible

reliable/unreliable

respectful/disrespectful

responsible/irresponsible

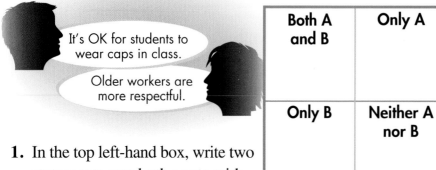

It's OK for students to wear caps in class.

Older workers are more respectful.

Both A and B	Only A
Only B	Neither A nor B

1. In the top left-hand box, write two statements you both agree with.
2. In the top right-hand box, write two statements A agrees with, but B doesn't.
3. In the bottom left-hand box, write two statements B agrees with, but A doesn't.
4. In the bottom right-hand box, write two statements neither of you agrees with.

Grammar Talk: Agreement and Disagreement

Al thinks that coming to work late is irresponsible, **and I do too.**
Al thinks that many people are unreliable, **and so do I.**
Al doesn't think that young people are more flexible, **and neither do I.**
Al doesn't think that young people are reliable, **and I don't either.**
Al thinks that older workers are more responsible, **but I don't.**
Al doesn't think that young workers learn more quickly, **but I do.**

In the first sentence, what does too *mean? What is the difference between* neither *and* either? *How are the last two sentences different?*

Activity A Look at the sentences in the grammar box. Tell your partner if you agree or disagree with what Al thinks.

Al thinks that older workers are more responsible, and I do too.

Activity B **Class Chat Follow-Up** Look at the chart you made in the Class Chat. In your notebook, write sentences about the opinions.

Mariano thinks it's OK to wear a cap in class, but I don't.

Pronunciation Target • Contrasting Sounds *th/th* and *ch/sh*

Make a chart with these headings in your notebook:

<u>th</u>ink   <u>th</u>at   <u>ch</u>ess   <u>sh</u>ould

🎧 *Repeat the words after your teacher. Notice the difference between the two* th *sounds and between the* ch *and* sh *sounds.*

Listen to your teacher or the audio. Write the words in the correct column.
The sound may be at the beginning, middle, or end.

Activity C   With your group, write a possible cause of each conflict below.
Discuss possible solutions for each conflict.

1. An older and younger worker argue
   about which radio station to listen to.

   <u>The younger worker wants to listen to rap music,</u>

   <u>but the older one wants traditional music.</u>

   I think they should turn
   the radio off.

   I do too.

   I don't. I think they should
   listen to one station in the morning
   and a different one in the
   afternoon.

2. An older worker doesn't like the way a young worker talks.

   _____

3. A young worker thinks an older worker is inflexible.

   _____

TASK 2: Write a Conversation

Adults of all ages work together or attend ESL classes together.
Sometimes conflicts happen because of different interests. As a
class, brainstorm conflicts that may happen and write them on
the board. Write a short conversation about one of these conflicts.
Share your conversation with your group.

> Younger students want to study
> about getting jobs, but older
> students don't.

	Vanessa:	Who cares about Columbus? I need to write a resume to get a job!
	Jean:	It's important to understand history!
	Vanessa:	History won't help me get a job!
	Jean:	But history will help you understand life!

Choose one conversation to share. As a class, answer these questions:
What is the problem? Who do you agree with? Explain your answer.

Sports to Play and Watch

◆ Decide which physical activities you like
◆ Learn about women in sports in the US

benefits
likely
self-discipline
sportsmanship
team

Have you or has anyone in your family ever participated in sports? Which ones?

◆ **Reading Tip** Mina's daughter wants to join the basketball team. She brings home a letter from school that describes the benefits of participation in sports. Focusing on specific information as you read can help you understand. As you read the letter, count how many benefits are mentioned.

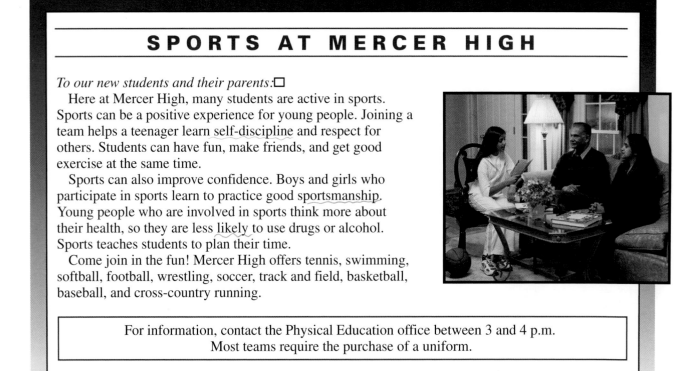

SPORTS AT MERCER HIGH

To our new students and their parents:☐

Here at Mercer High, many students are active in sports. Sports can be a positive experience for young people. Joining a team helps a teenager learn self-discipline and respect for others. Students can have fun, make friends, and get good exercise at the same time.

Sports can also improve confidence. Boys and girls who participate in sports learn to practice good sportsmanship. Young people who are involved in sports think more about their health, so they are less likely to use drugs or alcohol. Sports teaches students to plan their time.

Come join in the fun! Mercer High offers tennis, swimming, softball, football, wrestling, soccer, track and field, basketball, baseball, and cross-country running.

For information, contact the Physical Education office between 3 and 4 p.m.
Most teams require the purchase of a uniform.

Talk or Write

1. What is the main idea of the letter?
2. What are the supporting ideas?

Make a chart in your notebook. Write the main idea at the top of the page.

Write the supporting ideas under the main idea.

In the US   Women in US Sports

Not many years ago, very few women in the US participated in competitive sports. Now, however, many girls and women compete. It's common for girls to join softball, basketball, and soccer teams, as well as individual sports like gymnastics. In 1972, the federal government passed a law that says schools may not discriminate against girls in sports. Since that time, more and more girls have participated in school sports. Women's professional sports have also gained popularity. Although men's professional sports continue to be more popular, many people enjoy watching women's soccer, basketball, and volleyball. The growing popularity of women's sports can be seen in other countries, too. Every year the Olympics add more events for women, and all new Olympic sports must allow women to compete.

Vocabulary

Repeat these words after your teacher. Talk about their meanings. Write the words in your notebook. With a partner, write a sentence using each word.

challenge/challenging
compete/competitive
fitness
individual
risky
team

discriminate

Idiom Watch!
meet someone halfway

☛ **Compare Cultures**   Women and girls play all of these sports in the US. Do they play them in your home country? Check "yes" or "no" for each sport on the charts below. Share your information with the class, and write what you've learned in a class chart.

Sports	basketball	soccer	softball	tennis
Yes				
No				

Sports	swimming	golf	volleyball	track and field
Yes				
No				

Activity A   Annie's grandfather doesn't want her to join the basketball team. He thinks that Annie needs to spend time with her family. How can he and Annie meet halfway? In your group, discuss possible solutions. Share your ideas with the class. Role-play a conversation between them.

Activity B   With your group, make a chart like this one. Write 10 activities in the first column. Walk around the class, asking your classmates if they watch, play, or don't like each activity. Write one name in each box.

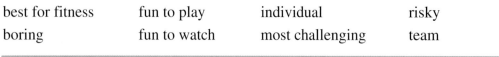

Activity	Watches	Plays	Doesn't Like
soccer	Nasrin	Robbie	Teruko

When you finish, write sentences about your classmates.

Robbie likes to play soccer, but Teruko doesn't.

Activity C   In your notebook, make several idea maps. Put the name of a sport in each center circle. Put these words in the outer circles of the sports that they describe. Use all the words. Share your idea maps with your group.

best for fitness	fun to play	individual	risky
boring	fun to watch	most challenging	team

Activity D   Ask your partner these questions and take notes on the answers.
1. Do you like to watch risky activities on TV? Which ones?
2. Do you like to play individual sports? Which ones?
3. Do you enjoy challenges? Give an example.
4. Is fitness important to you? Why?

Now meet with a different classmate and talk about your partner.

TASK 3: Give a Presentation

Choose a sport, activity, or hobby that you like. Use the plan below to prepare a short presentation for your group. Tell how to do the activity. Tell why you like it. Use a visual aid, such as a picture, a diagram, or equipment.

1. Name of activity
2. Visual aid
3. Step-by-step instructions
4. Why you like it

Presentation of Community Classes

Find out about classes in your community. Follow these steps:

Get Ready

Research classes that are available in your community.

1. Choose an age group that you are interested in: youth, adults, parents of young children, or the elderly.
2. Ask for written information from schools, churches, or cultural centers that offer classes for the group that you chose.
3. Bring brochures to class.

Do the Work

Work in small groups. Students who are interested in the same age group should work together.

1. Choose activities and classes from the brochures that would be interesting for people in the age group that you chose.
2. Put the information onto one page, including name of organization, place, dates, times, and fees.

Present

Present the information to the class. Each member of the group should present part of the information. After you listen to other groups, ask questions about the activities.

One Step Up

In a small group, create a community organization that fulfills an important need. For example, you could create a center that offers recreational after-school activities for teenagers. You could also form a group that organizes outings to parks for mothers and their young children. Make a brochure that tells the name of the organization, describes the resources that it offers, and lists the schedule of activities.

Writing Extension Write a short letter to a local organization, park service, or community center asking them to offer a class in something you're interested in. Explain what you want them to offer and why you think people would be interested in it.

✐▱ Technology Extra

Gather your information into a class book to share with others. Each group should type in the information for the age group they chose. Use graphics if possible. Print, laminate, and bind the book or put the pages into a binder with plastic sheet covers. Display the book in the classroom.

Smoothing Things Over

◆ **Vocabulary** Conflicts and resolutions

◆ **Language** Past continuous and simple past • Direct speech

◆ **Pronunciation** Stress in negative vs. affirmative statements
  • Syllable stress

◆ **Culture** Personal space and public behavior

Think about a misunderstanding that you had. Tell what happened.

Jae Lee, a 27-year-old from Korea, is talking to his friend, Koji, before English class. Jae Lee has lived in the US for many years. Although he speaks English very well, he sometimes has communication problems for other reasons.

Think and Talk

1. What do you see in the picture?
2. What do you see in this photo that might cause misunderstandings?
3. What happens when people misunderstand each other?
4. How do you feel about the way people are acting in this photo?

What's Your Opinion? In the photo, the instructor has his hand on a student's shoulder. Is this OK? Explain your answer.

Gather Your Thoughts   People often use body language and gestures to communicate. Think of examples of body language and gestures. Show the body language or gestures to your group and discuss what they mean to you.

Tell about a misunderstanding that happened because of body language or a gesture. Choose one example of a misunderstanding and make a chart like this one. Write the story in the boxes.

Expectation	Gesture/ Body Language	Misunderstanding	Resolution
I expected the teacher to be formal.	The teacher was sitting on the desk.	I didn't think that she was a good teacher.	She explained that many classrooms in this country are informal.

Vocabulary

Repeat these words after your teacher. Talk about their meanings. Write the words in your notebook. With a partner, write a sentence using each word.

expect/expectation
misunderstand/ misunderstanding
offend/offensive
resolve/resolution

body language
concerned
gesture

Idiom Watch!
smooth things over

What's the Problem?   Language differences can cause misunderstandings between people. What else can cause misunderstandings? Think or talk with a partner.

Setting Goals   Think about things you want to be able to do to communicate well. Which goals are most important to you? Rank them from 1 (most important) to 6.

_____ **a.** understand expectations in social situations in the US

_____ **b.** explain reasons for conflicts

_____ **c.** apologize for mistakes

_____ **d.** write a short letter

_____ **e.** understand and describe gestures and body language

_____ **f.** another goal:

Which was the most important goal for your class? Tally your answers. Talk about your most important goals.

Body Language

◆ Understand how body language can cause miscommunication
◆ Use past continuous and simple past

Body language is an important form of communication. Have you ever been offended by someone's body language? What happened?

◆ **Reading Tip** Thinking about a picture or an illustration can help you prepare for what you are going to read. Jae Lee is concerned about a problem with his neighbor. He is e-mailing his friend for advice. Look at the photo of Jae Lee and his neighbor. What do you think he is concerned about?

back away from

embarrassed

next-door neighbor

offend

Idiom Watch!

*throw your arms
around someone*

> Reply   Reply All   Forward

Koji,
What's up, my friend? I need your advice. My next-door neighbor is a woman about my age. She's single and she lives alone. I haven't talked to her very much, but she seems nice. Yesterday, I was watering my lawn when I saw her puppy running down the middle of the street. I ran after it and caught it. My neighbor wasn't home, so I put the dog in my backyard until she came home from work. When I returned the dog, she said, "Oh, you're so wonderful!" Then, she threw her arms around me! It surprised me so much that I backed away from her. I'm afraid that I offended her, but I'm too embarrassed to talk to her about it. What do you think?
Jae Lee

Talk or Write

1. Why is Jae Lee writing this e-mail?
2. Why do you think the neighbor hugged Jae Lee?
3. Why does Jae Lee think that he offended his neighbor?
4. Why is Jae Lee embarrassed to talk to her about it?

What's Your Opinion? Do you think that Jae Lee should talk to his neighbor about the misunderstanding? Why or why not?

Group Chat Look at the words in the Vocabulary box. Think about when you have seen someone do each action. What was happening? Why did the person do the action? Tell your group.

My mom asked my brother why he didn't do his homework. He shrugged because he couldn't think of a reason.

Make a chart like this one. Use all of the words from the Vocabulary box. Answer the questions with information from people in your group.

Action	What was happening?	Why did he/she _____?
shrug	My mom was talking to my brother.	He couldn't think of an answer.

Vocabulary

Repeat these words after your teacher. Talk about their meanings. Write the words in your notebook. With a partner, write a sentence using each word.

bow
nudge
shrug
slouch
stare
whisper
whistle
wink

Grammar Talk: Statements with Past Continuous and Simple Past

Jae Lee **was bowing** to his Tae Kwon Do teacher.
He **fell** over.

Sarah **was slouching** in her chair.
Her father **told** her to sit up straight.

Sam and Koji **were staring** at the pretty girl.
She **walked** away from them.

Which actions were continuous? Which actions interrupted the other ones? How do you form the past continuous?

Pronunciation Target • Stress in Negative vs. Affirmative Statements

🎧 *Listen to your teacher or the audio. Repeat these sentences:*

They were **star**ing.   They **weren't star**ing.
He was **whist**ling.   He **wasn't whist**ling.

In affirmative statements, was and were are not stressed, but they are stressed in negative statements.

Activity A 🎧 Listen to your teacher or the audio. In your notebook, write the sentences that you hear. Listen for negative and affirmative statements.

Activity B **Group Chat Follow-Up** Look at the chart from your Group Chat on page 25. In your notebook, use each of the words from the Vocabulary list and the information from your chart to write sentences.

My brother was talking to my mom. He shrugged when she asked him a question.

Activity C Look at the following situations with your group. Take turns asking "why" questions about each situation. Have a contest to see which group can think of the most answers to each question.

Why were the children staring at the woman?

Maybe the woman was beautiful.

Maybe she was wearing a funny hat.

1. The children were staring at the woman.
2. The employee was slouching behind the counter.
3. The employee was shrugging when his boss was talking to him.
4. The student was bowing.
5. The woman was backing away from the man.
6. The girls were nudging each other and whispering.

Activity D Look at the sentences. Discuss what each person thought or felt.

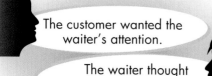

The customer wanted the waiter's attention.

The waiter thought whistling was offensive.

1. The customer whistled at the waiter.
2. The Tae Kwon Do student didn't bow to his teacher.
3. The woman nudged someone out of the way when she was shopping.
4. A man winked at a woman that he didn't know very well.

TASK 1: Write a Letter

Write a letter to your teacher or to another student. Tell about a time when you or someone you know communicated with body language. In your letter, answer these questions: Where were you? What were you doing? Did the action cause miscommunication? Why or why not? In your last sentence, ask for advice or an opinion.

A friendly letter usually looks like the picture to the right.

May 15, 2004

Dear Koji,
_____
_____
_____

Sincerely,
Jae Lee

A Simple Apology

◆ Make apologies and give explanations
◆ Use direct speech

scan = read quickly

Have you ever apologized to anyone in English? Explain the situation.

◆ **Reading Tip** The best way to find specific information is to read quickly. Scan the form below to find the day of the week that was circled.

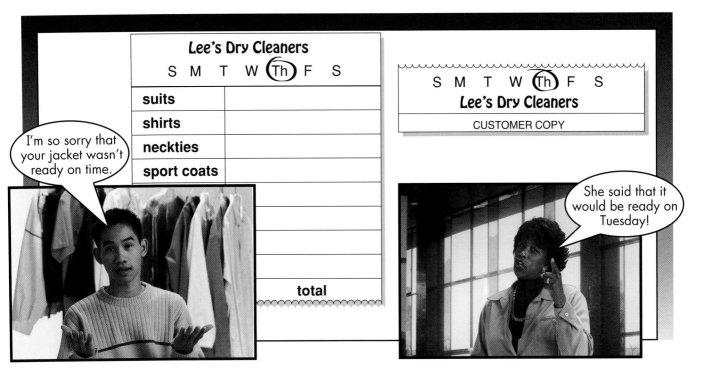

Talk or Write
1. Why was the woman angry?
2. What day did the woman think her jacket would be ready?
3. What do you think caused the miscommunication?
4. Whose fault was it?
5. Why did Jae Lee apologize?

What's Your Opinion? People often apologize so that other people won't be angry. Should people apologize even if something isn't their fault? Can an apology resolve a problem? Explain your answer.

Group Chat   People often have to apologize for things that happen at work. With your group, brainstorm problems that can happen at work because of miscommunication. Write about one problem in each circle. Near the circle, write what someone might say because of the problem.

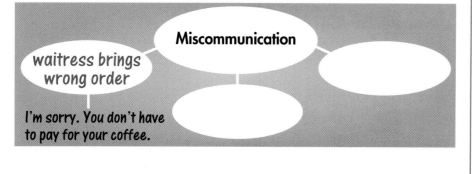

Vocabulary

Repeat these words after your teacher. Talk about their meanings. Write the words in your notebook. With a partner, write a sentence using each word.

excuse me

forgive me

pardon me

apologize

apology

fault

mix-up

Grammar Talk: Direct Speech

Jae Lee said, **"I'**m sorry that your clothes aren't ready. Please excuse the misunderstanding**."**

Valerie said, **"P**lease forgive me for being late. I was talking to an important customer**."**

These sentences show exactly what the people said. Where is the comma in each sentence? Where are the quotation marks? Notice that each quote begins with a capital letter.

Vocabulary Plus
Pardon me, forgive me and *excuse me* are usually followed by *for* + verb + *-ing:* Excuse me **for being** late.

Pronunciation Target • Syllable Stress

🎧 *Listen to your teacher or the audio. Repeat and emphasize the stressed syllables.*

I'm **sor**ry.   Please for**give** me.   I misunder**stood** you.

Ex**cuse** me.   I want to a**pol**ogize.

Stressed syllables are longer than unstressed syllables.

Activity A   With your partner, practice complaining and making apologies. Then create a conversation and practice saying it for your group.

Activity B **Group Chat Follow-Up** Look at the sentences that you wrote in your Group Chat idea map. Write them in direct speech in your notebook.

The manager said, "I'm sorry. You don't have to pay for your coffee."

Activity C In your notebook, unscramble the words in each sentence. Work with a partner. Remember to use a comma and quotation marks.

1. forgot / sorry / the / she / to / soda / I'm / said / bring / that / I
   She said, "I'm sorry that I forgot to bring the soda."

2. you / so / me / said / long / pardon / on / she / for / hold / keeping

3. hours / sorry / now / visiting / I'm / but / he / over / said / are

4. for / said / package / your / with / forgive / he / please / us / mix-up / the

Activity D Look at the pictures. With your partner, practice making apologies using the vocabulary words. Think of as many apologies as you can.

> I'm sorry that I misunderstood the homework.

> Forgive me for coming to class late.

TASK 2: Write a Conversation

Look at the following list of problems that could happen at work. In pairs, write a conversation with an appropriate apology and a short explanation. Practice the apologies in pairs.

• A waitress brings the wrong order to a customer.

Customer: Excuse me, this isn't what I ordered. I wanted wheat bread.

Waitress: I'm sorry for the misunderstanding. I thought you said white.

• An employee comes to a meeting at the wrong time.
• A college student goes to the wrong class.
• A pizza place delivers the wrong pizza.

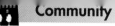 **Community**

In Public

◆ Describe public behaviors
◆ Learn about American public behavior

What things do people do in public that bother you?

◆ **Listening Tip** 🎧 Thinking about what you already know about a topic can help you understand what you hear. What do you know about martial arts classes? Listen to your teacher or the audio. Listen to the whole conversation once. Then read the questions and listen again. You can read the words on page 118.

give yourself a break

goof around

make a fool of myself

know better

Sarah is telling Jae Lee and Koji about something that she did in Tae Kwon Do class that bothered her instructor.

Talk or Write
1. What was Sarah doing in her Tae Kwon Do class?
2. What did the teacher do?
3. What advice did Jae Lee give her?
4. How is a martial arts class different from an aerobics class?
5. Why did Jae Lee tell Sarah about his experience with his neighbor?

In the US Personal Space and Public Behavior

"Personal space" is the distance between two people that seems comfortable. In the US, this distance is about two feet. If you stand or sit too close to someone, the person will feel uncomfortable. If you stand much farther away than two feet, the person will probably move closer to you.

"Public behavior" is the way people act in places like supermarkets and restaurants. When people in the US are shopping, they stand in line to get help, or they take a number. They think it is rude to cut in line. Also, if they want to reach past another customer, they do not touch the other person. People usually say, "Excuse me," and wait for the other person to move. In restaurants, it is impolite to call the waiter by snapping your fingers, whistling, or saying "Psst." People raise one hand and wait for the waiter to see them, or they say "Excuse me" to get the waiter's attention.

☛ **Compare Cultures** Think about how people behave in public places in your home country. Make a diagram like this one. Write the name of your home country in one circle. Write US in the other circle. Choose a public place for the title.

Vocabulary

Repeat these words after your teacher. Talk about their meanings. Write the words in your notebook. With a partner, write a sentence using each word.

- aggressive
- impatient
- impolite
- interrupt
- polite
- rude
- snap your fingers

Idiom Watch!
cut in line

Market

Spain	cashier thanks customer	US
customers stand in a group and ask who is last		customers stand in line

---

Activity A Sit in a circle. Tell the student next to you an idea you have about public behavior. That person tells the next student what you said, and adds another idea. The third student tells the fourth student exactly what students 1 and 2 said.

When you have gone around the circle once, write down what each student said in direct speech. Check to see if everyone in your group wrote exactly the same sentences, including punctuation.

I think it's rude to interrupt.

Tony said, "It's rude to interrupt." I think that cheating is dishonest.

Tony said, "It's rude to interrupt." Linh said, "Cheating is dishonest." I think that pushing is aggressive.

Activity B Discuss these pictures with your partner. Describe the way the people are behaving. For example, are they being rude, polite, aggressive, impatient, friendly, etc.? Explain your opinion.

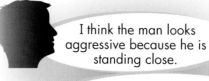

I think the man looks aggressive because he is standing close.

I think he's friendly because he's smiling.

TASK 3: Write a Story

Make a chart like this one on the board. With the class, list some differences between the way people in the US act in these places and the way people act in your home country.

	Bus	Supermarket	Movie Theater	School
US	sit in empty seat don't look at people			
Other Countries	sit next to someone OK to look at people			

You can add other places to your chart, such as *Park* or *Bank*. Discuss what communication problems might be caused by these differences. In small groups, tell about your experiences with any of these problems.

Choose the most interesting story and write it on poster paper. If no one has a story to share, create one as a group. Share the story with the class. Include what people said. Together, correct the past-tense verbs and direct speech.

I think many people in this country are not friendly when they take the bus. They don't want to talk to anybody. One time I got on the bus to go downtown. There was an empty seat next to this guy, and I asked him, "Can I sit here?" He just turned his head and stared out the window. He didn't even answer me. That's rude!

Write a Skit

Write a skit about a misunderstanding. Follow these steps:

skit

Get Ready

1. In your group, write a skit that demonstrates a misunderstanding between two people. Don't try to solve the problem.
2. You can bring things to class to make your skit more interesting. For example, bring a baseball and talk about a broken window, bring a pizza box and talk about delivering to the wrong house, bring a broken clock and talk about being late.
3. Plan your body language. Include some of the actions from the Vocabulary box on page 25. Memorize your lines.

Do the Work

Use a work sheet like the one to the right to plan and write your skit. Each person should say at least four sentences. Choose two group members to perform the skit.

Title:_____

Place:_____

Names of characters:_____ and _____

Problem:_____

Conversation:

A:_____ B:_____

A:_____ B:_____

A:_____ B:_____

A:_____ B:_____

Present

Present your skit. After each skit is presented, decide how to solve the problem. Work in pairs. Write your solutions on large strips of paper. Tape them on the board. As a class, discuss each solution.

Writing Extension Choose one of the communication problems from the skits and write a paragraph explaining the problem. Tell which solution you think is best and explain why. Remember to indent and stay within the margins.

Technology Extra

Use the following key words to do an Internet search: "cultural diversity," "cultural conflicts," "body language." Choose an article to print and share it with your group.

Better Safe Than Sorry

Making Our Lives Safe

Work/School 1   Home 2   Community 3

◆ **Vocabulary** Safety words

◆ **Language** Past-tense questions and answers • Sentences with *when, before,* and *after*

◆ **Pronunciation** Past-tense endings • Stress on important words

◆ **Culture** Neighborhood safety

Where have you seen a neighborhood like this?

Miguel Jimenez, a 19-year-old from Nicaragua, lives in Rochester, New York, with his parents and younger brother and sisters. Miguel has been worried about safety at his job, at home, and in his neighborhood.

Think and Talk

1. What do you see in the photograph?
2. What do you think Miguel is worried about?
3. What caused the safety problems in his neighborhood?
4. What concerns do you have about your safety?

concerns

What's Your Opinion? Many people notice things that make their homes, workplaces, or neighborhoods unsafe, but they don't do or say anything. Can you explain why? Are those good or bad reasons for not doing anything?

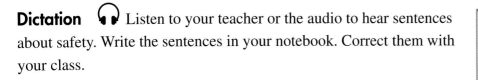

Dictation 🎧 Listen to your teacher or the audio to hear sentences about safety. Write the sentences in your notebook. Correct them with your class.

Gather Your Thoughts In groups, brainstorm safety problems that you have at home, at work, and in your community. Categorize them in an idea map like the one below. Decide which problem in each place is most important. Put a check by that problem.

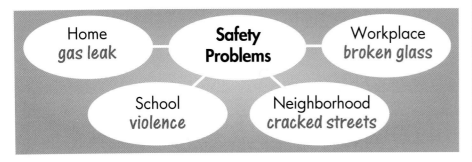

What's the Problem? What causes each of the safety problems you listed? What can be done to prevent these problems? Think or talk with a partner.

Setting Goals Think about things you want to be able to do to be safe. Which goals are most important to you? Rank the goals in order from 1 (most important) to 6.

_____ **a.** report an accident

_____ **b.** prevent injuries at work

_____ **c.** make my home safe

_____ **d.** help make my neighborhood safe

_____ **e.** report a crime

_____ **f.** another goal: _____

Which was the most important goal for your class? Tally your answers. Talk about your most important goals.

Vocabulary

Repeat these words after your teacher. Talk about their meanings. Write the words in your notebook. With a partner, write a sentence using each word.

cause/cause
injure/injury
poison/poisonous
prevent/prevention
rob/robbery
slip/slippery
suspect/suspicious

Idiom Watch!
*better safe
than sorry*

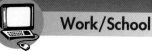

Safety on the Job

◆ Be able to report workplace accidents
◆ Use past-tense questions and answers

fracture
grill
splatter
treat
wound

Do you know someone who was injured at work? What happened?

◆ **Reading Tip** When you read a form to find specific information, it's not necessary to read every word. Look quickly through the form for key words. Read the questions below this accident report form. Then scan for the answers.

Accident Report Form Please print.

Name: Miguel Jimenez   Social Security #: 546-73-2228
Address: 224 Olive St.   Date of birth: 10/17/83
City/Zip: Rochester, NY 14614   Job title: cook

Date/time accident happened: 10/7/03 12:30 PM
Date/time accident treated: 10/7/03 12:40 PM
Date/time accident reported: 10/7/03 2:00 PM

Type of Injury: Indicate with an X

Fracture ____ Bruise ____ Burn X Sprain ____ Cut ____ Open wound ____
Internal ____ Head ____ Spinal ____ Dental ____ Other _____

Part of Body Injured: Indicate right (R) or left (L)

Ankle ____ Arm ____ Back ____ Chest ____ Elbow ____ Foot ____ Hand L
Head ____ Knee ____ Leg ____ Neck ____ Shoulder ____ Wrist ____ Other ____

Describe where and how the accident happened.

I was standing near the grill, and I knocked over a bottle of oil. It spilled onto the grill.
The hot oil splattered from the grill and burned my left hand.

> After the nurse treated my burn, I filled out an accident form for my manager.

Talk or Write

1. When did the accident happen?
2. What was Miguel's injury?
3. What caused the accident?
4. What can workers and managers do to prevent accidents at a restaurant?

What's Your Opinion? Miguel knows that there are safety problems at work that need to be fixed. He's an employee, not the boss. Is it right for him to tell his boss that things need to be changed? Explain your answer.

Partner Chat With your partner, write more ideas about safety problems at work. Make an idea map like the one below. Ask your teacher for help with words you don't know. Share with the class.

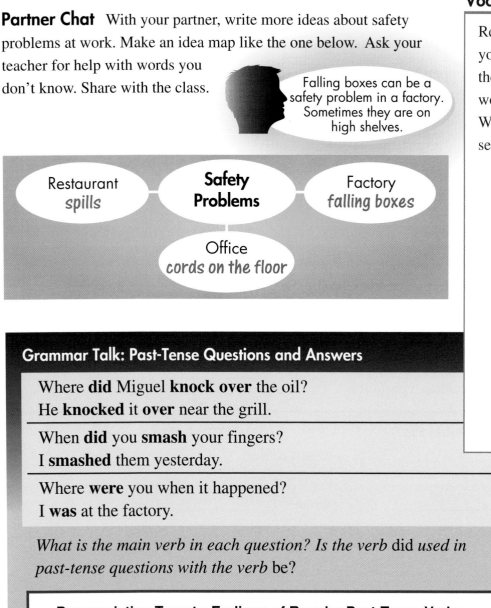

Falling boxes can be a safety problem in a factory. Sometimes they are on high shelves.

Restaurant
spills

Safety Problems

Factory
falling boxes

Office
cords on the floor

Vocabulary

Repeat these words after your teacher. Talk about their meanings. Write the words in your notebook. With a partner, write a sentence using each word.

knock over

smash

treat

trip over

bruise

fracture

shock

spill

sprain

wound

Grammar Talk: Past-Tense Questions and Answers

Where **did** Miguel **knock over** the oil?
He **knocked** it **over** near the grill.

When **did** you **smash** your fingers?
I **smashed** them yesterday.

Where **were** you when it happened?
I **was** at the factory.

What is the main verb in each question? Is the verb did *used in past-tense questions with the verb* be?

Pronunciation Target • Endings of Regular Past-Tense Verbs

🎧 *Listen to your teacher or the audio. Repeat these words: smash**ed**, bruis**ed**, report**ed**. Notice that each one ends with a different sound: /t/, /d/, or /ed/.*

Now listen to your teacher or the audio say the past tense of the words in the Vocabulary box.

Activity A Tell your partner about a workplace accident. You can imagine an accident if you don't know about a real one. Remember to include the place, the time, the people involved, and what happened. Describe any injuries. Have your partner listen to you say the **-ed** at the end of your verbs.

One Step Up
Write your story.

Activity B Tell your partner your story from Activity A. Then ask your partner these questions about your story.

1. Where did the accident happen?
2. When did it happen?
3. Who was hurt?
4. What happened?

If your partner can't answer the questions, tell the story again. Then listen to your partner's story. Ask for more information to help you answer the questions.

One Step Up

With a partner, role-play reporting your accident to a supervisor. The supervisor should ask questions like those in Activity B.

Activity C **Partner Chat Follow-Up** Look at your Partner Chat idea map on page 37. Write sentences using information from the circles.

Falling boxes are a safety problem at factories.

TASK 1: Complete an Accident Report Form

Use your story to fill out this accident report form.

Accident Report Form   Please print.

Name: _____   Social Security #: _____

Address: _____   Date of birth: _____

City/Zip: _____   Job title: _____

Date/time accident happened: _____

Date/time accident treated: _____

Date/time accident reported: _____

Type of Injury: Indicate with an X.

Fracture _____ Bruise _____ Burn _____ Sprain _____ Cut _____ Open wound _____

Internal _____ Head _____ Spinal _____ Dental _____ Other _____

Part of Body Injured: Indicate right (R) or left (L).

Ankle _____ Arm _____ Back _____ Chest _____ Elbow _____ Foot _____ Hand _____

Head _____ Knee _____ Leg _____ Neck _____ Shoulder _____ Wrist _____ Other _____

Describe where and how the accident happened.

_____

_____

_____

Safety at Home

- ◆ Learn ways to make your home safer
- ◆ Use sentences with *when, before,* and *after*

Do you know how to prevent fires in your home? Give some examples.

- ◆ **Reading Tip** Before you read something, it helps to predict, or guess, what it will be about. Look at the photo of Miguel and the title of the brochure. Can you predict what Miguel will do with the information in the brochure?

escape route

smoke detector

smother

space heater

valuables

Fire Safety in Your Home

Here are some things you can do to be safe in your home.

- ▶ Draw a floor plan with at least two ways to escape from every room. Show important details such as doors, stairs, and windows that can be used as escape routes.
- ▶ Use smoke detectors. Check them every month. Change batteries at least once a year.
- ▶ Always sleep with the bedroom doors closed to keep heat and smoke out of bedrooms. If there is a fire, touch the door before opening it. If it feels hot, keep it closed! Go out a window.
- ▶ In a fire, time is very important. Just get out! Don't look for pets or valuables before you leave the house. Call 911 after you leave the house.
- ▶ Turn off space heaters before going to bed or leaving the house.

- ▶ Keep things that can burn easily away from cooking areas.
- ▶ If grease catches fire, don't throw water on it. Carefully slide a lid over the pan. Then turn off the burner.
- ▶ If a toaster or other appliance smokes, unplug it immediately and have it repaired. Replace cracked electrical cords. Don't put cords under rugs.

Talk or Write

1. What important details should be in an escape plan?
2. How often should you check smoke detectors?
3. When should you turn off space heaters?
4. What should you do if grease catches fire?
5. When should you replace electrical cords?

Group Chat After Miguel's accident, he became concerned about safety. Most people can remember a time when they didn't feel safe. Talk to several classmates about a time when they were concerned about safety at home. Take notes about their answers on your chart.

Vocabulary

Repeat these words after your teacher. Talk about their meanings. Write the words in your notebook. With a partner, write a sentence using each word.

escape route
fire extinguisher
smoke detector

lock up
plug in
put away
replace
unplug

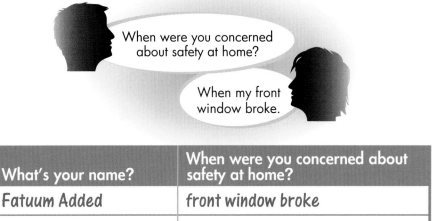

When were you concerned about safety at home?

When my front window broke.

What's your name?	When were you concerned about safety at home?
Fatuum Added	front window broke

Grammar Talk: Sentences with *when*, *before*, and *after*

when	I was scared **when** the smoke detector went off.
	When the smoke detector went off, I was scared.
before	Turn the heater off **before** you go to bed.
	Before you go to bed, turn the heater off.
after	They called the firefighters **after** they left the house.
	After they left the house, they called the firefighters.

Idiom Watch!
go off

A clause with when, before, *or* after *is not a complete thought. It is only part of a sentence. What can you say about the position of these clauses in a sentence? When do you need to use a comma with these clauses?*

Pronunciation Target • Stress on Important Words
🎧 I was **scared** when the **smoke** detector went **off**.
Do **not** place **cords** under **rugs**.

In English, important words are stressed. This means that they are **longer** *than unstressed words.*

Activity A 🎧 Listen to your teacher or the audio. Write the sentences that you hear in your notebook. Write *T (true)* or *F (false)* after each sentence.

Activity B Match the words in the left column to the safety rules in the right column.

<u>_d_</u> **1.** paint   **a.** keep in locked cabinet

_____ **2.** smoke detector   **b.** connect to the wall

_____ **3.** cleaning supplies   **c.** be sure you put them out

_____ **4.** iron   **d.** keep in closed container

_____ **5.** bookcase   **e.** replace batteries regularly

_____ **6.** cigarettes   **f.** unplug when not in use

Activity C **Group Chat Follow-Up** Look at your Group Chat chart on page 40. Write sentences about when you and your classmates were concerned about safety.

<u>Fatuum was concerned when her front window broke.</u>

Remember?
Use *should* to give advice.

Activity D In your groups, ask and answer these questions. Begin your answers with "You should. . . ." Use *when, before,* or *after* in your answers. What should you do . . .

1. before you plug in a hair dryer?   **4.** after a fire starts?

2. when you feel an earthquake?   **5.** after you use paint?

3. before a big storm?   **6.** after you use a ladder?

TASK 2: Design an Escape Route

Look at the escape route. Then design one for your home for a fire or other emergency. Draw a map with doors, stairs, and windows. Explain your escape route to your group. Write about how to make your home safer.

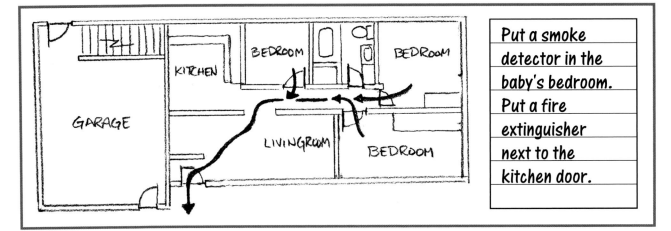

Put a smoke detector in the baby's bedroom. Put a fire extinguisher next to the kitchen door.

At the Bus Stop

◆ Learn how to make your neighborhood safer
◆ Give advice about neighborhood safety

Do you know someone who has been a victim of a crime? What happened?

◆ **Listening Tip**  Look at the photo to predict what happened to the couple. Then listen to your teacher or the audio. You can read the words on page 118.

Miguel witnessed a purse snatching on his way to work. Officer Murphy is talking to him about the crime.

Talk or Write

1. How did the purse snatching happen?
2. Who were the victims?
3. What did the suspects look like?
4. Why do you think the people went inside?

What's Your Opinion? Was it a good idea for Miguel to run after the suspects? Explain your answer.

Idiom Watch!

get a good look at

Vocabulary

Repeat these words after your teacher. Talk about their meanings. Write the words in your notebook. With a partner, write a sentence using each word.

mugged

stolen

stranger

victim

witness

Idiom Watch!

break in

keep an eye on

get to know

In the US   Keeping Neighborhoods Safe

In the US, some people make their neighborhoods safer by getting to know their neighbors. People introduce themselves when new neighbors move in. They ask each other to keep an eye on their homes when they travel. They may ask neighbors to pick up their newspapers and mail so strangers won't know that they are away. Some neighborhoods form Neighborhood Watch groups with the help of the police. In these groups, neighbors meet and work together with the police to report problems in the neighborhood.

☞ **Compare Cultures** How is your neighborhood in the US different from your neighborhood in your home country? Are you safer in the US, or were you safer before coming here? Tell the class.

Activity A   With your class, talk about how to be safer in your neighborhood. Write ideas on a chart like this one. Post your chart on the wall of your classroom or somewhere else in your school.

Protect Myself	Protect Neighborhood
Walk quickly at night.	Leave outdoor lights on.

Activity B Walk around. Pretend that your classmates are your neighbors. Choose one situation to role-play with each student. Continue until you role-play four of the five situations.

Could I borrow a hammer? I lost mine.

1. Borrow something from your neighbor.
2. Ask your neighbor to keep an eye on your house while you're away.
3. Invite a neighbor over for coffee or tea.
4. Ask a neighbor where to shop for something.
5. Ask your neighbor to pick up your mail and newspapers when you're away. Tell the neighbor how long you'll be gone.

One Step Up
Choose your favorite situation. Role-play it for the class with the partner you had for that situation.

Activity C Listen to your teacher or the audio. You will hear a telephone conversation between a man and a 911 operator. Work with a partner. Talk about the problem and the solution. Then choose one of these emergencies. Write, practice, and present another 911 conversation together.

911. What is your emergency?

My neighbor fell down our stairs, and he can't move.

1. Someone in your apartment building is having chest pains.
2. You smell gas coming from an empty apartment.
3. You see someone trying to break into your neighbor's house.

TASK 3: Make a Crime-Prevention Flyer

Work in a group. Imagine that you are a Neighborhood Watch group. Make a flyer that tells how to prevent common crimes. First, each group member will complete this chart. Then the group will choose ideas for the flyer.

Problem	Prevention
1. A woman is mugged while looking in her purse for the keys to her door.	*Take keys out of your purse before leaving your car.*
2. A thief breaks into a house when he sees newspapers in the front yard.	
3. Neighbors suspect a break-in, but they don't call the police.	
4. Someone starts selling drugs on a dark street corner.	
5. A thief reaches into the open window of a woman's car and grabs her purse.	

Make a Safety Poster

Make a safety poster for a place in your neighborhood or town. Follow these steps:

Get Ready

1. With your group, choose a workplace, school, park, or public building.
2. Study this safety poster that one class made.

Do the Work

1. Plan your poster. Use the Unit Project handout that your teacher will give you.
2. Give the poster a title.
3. Include illustrations, if possible. You can draw them, cut them from magazines or brochures, or find them on the Internet. You can include a drawing of an escape route.

Present

Present your poster to the class.

Playground Safety

- Use park equipment properly

- Stay out of the playground after dark

- Watch children at all times

Writing Extension Write a letter to the Mayor or the City Council about the place that you chose for your poster. Follow these steps:

1. In your first paragraph, tell about the place. Explain why it is important to you.
2. In your second paragraph, tell why the place is dangerous and explain your safety plan.
3. If you can, attach photos or illustrations of the problem and a small version of your poster. (See Technology Extra below.)

One Step Up
Ask for permission to put up your poster in the community.

✎💻 Technology Extra

Make a small version of your poster on the computer. Add graphics or clip art. Put a border around the rules. Print copies for everyone in your class.

Planning Ahead

Planning for Financial Security

Work/School 1 Home 2 Community 3

◆ **Vocabulary** Financial planning words

◆ **Language** Sentences with *because* • *Have to, must,* and *have got to*

◆ **Pronunciation** Choice intonation • Schwa in unstressed syllables

◆ **Culture** Saving for the future

What things can people do to have more financial security?

Olivia is 35 years old. She and her husband, Victor, live in a small rented house. She recently inherited some furniture from her grandmother. She is concerned about protecting her valuables, paying medical bills, and saving for the future.

Think and Talk

1. What do you see in the photo?
2. What can Olivia do to have more financial security?
3. What kinds of papers do you think she is looking at?
4. What concerns do you have about financial security?

> valuables
>
> coverage

What's Your Opinion? Sometimes when people apply for insurance, they don't tell the insurance company about a medical problem that they have. They are afraid that they won't get coverage. Do you think it's OK for a person to hide a medical problem from an insurance company in order to get coverage? Explain your answer.

Gather Your Thoughts Many people don't buy insurance. Use the expressions in the chart to talk about reasons why they don't. Write your ideas next to the expressions.

Vocabulary	Why don't people buy insurance?
financial security	*People don't think insurance will give them financial security.*
affordable coverage	
deductible amount	
monthly payments	
insurance agent	
eligible for coverage	

What's the Problem? What prevents people from having financial security? Think or talk with a partner.

Idiom Watch!
plan ahead

Setting Goals Insurance policies and savings accounts are important parts of financial planning. Which goals are most important to you? Rank them from 1 (most important) to 6.

_____ **a.** understand health insurance policies

_____ **b.** understand renters and home insurance policies

_____ **c.** learn names of medical specialists

_____ **d.** ask for information about savings accounts

_____ **e.** compare different kinds of savings accounts

_____ **f.** another goal: _____

Which was the most important goal for your class? Tally your answers. Talk about your most important goals. Explain your choices.

Vocabulary

Repeat these words after your teacher. Talk about their meanings. Write the words in your notebook. With a partner, write a sentence using each word.

agent
coverage
deductible
payments
policy
premium
security

afford
cover

affordable
eligible
financial

Vocabulary Plus

In your notebook, write these words across the top of a page: *Two-Syllable, Three-Syllable, Four-Syllable*. Listen to your teacher say the words in the Vocabulary box. Write each word in the correct column. Listen again, and underline the stressed syllables.

Decisions, Decisions!

◆ Understand how to interpret and choose health insurance
◆ Use sentences with *because*

dependents

network

preventive

recommend

treatment

What experiences have you had with health insurance? Are your experiences different in this country than they were in your home country? Explain your answer.

◆ **Reading Tip** Olivia received this memo from the Human Resources Department of her company. Focusing on why something was written can help you understand what you are reading. Scan the memo to see what it's about.

Health Insurance BENEFITS at Aptel, Inc.

If you are a full-time employee, you are eligible for medical benefits. When you sign up, you may choose individual or family coverage. Family coverage includes your spouse and unmarried children to age 19. Your unmarried dependents that are full-time college students are covered to age 25. Aptel pays for some of the cost of your medical coverage. The amount that you pay depends on the medical coverage that you choose. Aptel offers two health plans:

1. **Health Maintenance Organization (HMO)**
   This plan provides 100% coverage for most preventive care and medical treatment. You must use a network doctor as your Primary Care Physician. Your Primary Care Physician must recommend treatment. You will need to make small payments for visits and prescription drugs.

2. **Point-of-Service (POS)**
   This plan provides about 90% coverage for most preventive care and treatment within network. You can see any doctor you choose, but you will have higher payments when you use an out-of-network physician. Most out-of-network services are covered at 80% after deductibles are paid.

Talk or Write

1. What is the purpose of the memo?
2. Which family members are covered by the medical benefits?
3. What is a Primary Care Physician?
4. How are the two health plans similar? How are they different?

Partner Chat   Make an idea map like this one. Write the types of health care professionals in the circles. Why do people see these professionals? Discuss with your partner.

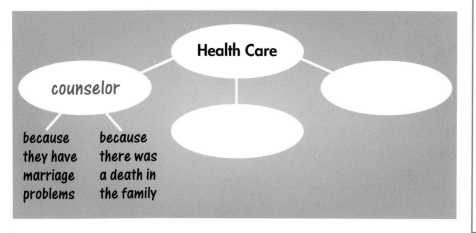

Vocabulary

Repeat these words after your teacher. Talk about their meanings. Write the words in your notebook. With a partner, write a sentence using each word.

acupuncturist/acupuncture

chiropractor/chiropractic

counselor/counseling

optometrist/vision

pediatrician/pediatric

Grammar Talk: Sentences with *because*

Avalon sees a chiropractor **because** she hurt her back in an accident.

Salvador couldn't afford counseling **because** his deductible was too high.

Maggie went to the optometrist **because** her vision was bad.

Each sentence uses the word because. *Is the underlined "because clause" a complete sentence? Is there a comma before* because?

Pronunciation Target • Choice Intonation

🎧 *Listen to your teacher or the audio.*
Is the deductible **five** hundred or **three** hundred?
Is this a **new** policy or an **old** policy?

When you offer a choice, both choices are stressed. However, the first choice is higher-pitched than the second one.

Activity A   Think of a choice for your classmates to make. Walk around the class. Offer your classmates the choice. Tell your group what most people chose.

Do you want chocolate or vanilla?

Activity B **Partner Chat Follow-Up** Look at the idea map from your Partner Chat. Using ideas from your idea map, write sentences in your notebook about someone you know. Use *because* in your sentences.

My mother goes to an acupuncturist because she has headaches.

Activity C Look at the reading on page 48. In your group, talk about the good points and bad points of each health plan. Make a choice between HMO and Point-of-Service. Students who choose HMO, stand on one side of the room. Students who choose Point-of-Service, stand on the other. Explain your decision.

> Do you like the HMO or Point-of-Service?

> I like Point-of-Service because I want to see my pediatrician. He knows my daughter's medical history.

Activity D Rank the following kinds of health-care coverage in order of importance to you. Number 1 is most important.

> I prefer the HMO because it's more affordable.

_____ dental checkup twice a year   _____ pediatric care   _____ surgery

_____ yearly medical checkup   _____ prescriptions   _____ hospital

_____ counseling services   _____ maternity care   _____ yearly vision exam

Go around your group and ask each member to list the three most important kinds of health insurance coverage. Which kinds were the most popular?

TASK 1: Compare Medical Insurance Plans

With your partner, compare deductibles and basic coverage of the following two medical insurance plans. The chart shows how much patients need to pay for each service. Use the information to make a choice between the two plans, and explain your choice to the class. Use *because* when you explain your choice.

	Health Guard Insurance Co.	Sana Delta Insurance Co.
Yearly deductible	$500	$1,200
Lifetime maximum	none	$1,000,000
Office visits	$15.00	$5.00
Yearly check-up	$30.00	$20.00
Emergency care	20%	$50.00
Hospital services	10%	none
X-rays	30%	20%
Maternity care	$15.00 each visit	20%
Prescription drugs	20%	none

Do you know anyone whose household belongings have been damaged or stolen? What happened?

belongings

damage

premium

theft

worth

◆ **Listening Tip** 🎧 Focusing on specific information can help you understand what you hear. Listen for the benefits of renters insurance that the agent describes. You can read the words on page 119.

Idiom Watch!
get back to you
talk it over

Olivia called an insurance agent because she's interested in protecting her household belongings. Victor didn't know about the appointment.

Talk or Write

1. What kind of insurance does Olivia want?
2. Does the landlord have to pay if your TV is stolen?
3. What kinds of belongings does renters insurance cover?
4. What kind of damage does the insurance cover?

water damage   fire and smoke   freezing of pipes

Tell your group if any of these things have happened to you or anyone you know. Decide which of these things are most likely to happen where you live. Explain your choices.

Make a pie chart. Color in more sections of the chart for situations that are more likely to happen to you. Color in fewer sections for situations that are less likely to happen to you. Share your pie chart with your group.

With a partner, write a sentence using each word.

antiques

belongings

valuables

damage

destroy

flood

hail

theft

vandalism/vandalize

Grammar Talk: Sentences with *must, have to,* and *have got to*

If you want replacement insurance, you **must** pay more.
You **must not** forget to pay your premiums on time.
Insurance companies **don't have to** cover natural disasters.
If someone vandalizes your car, you **have to** report it immediately.
I**'ve got to** keep my valuables in a safe place.

Notice that must *is never followed by* to. *How do you form the negatives of* must *and* have to? *Which expression is never used in the negative?*

Vocabulary Plus

The word *damage* is a noun and a verb.

Pronunciation Target • Schwa in Unstressed Syllables

🎧 *Listen to your teacher or the audio. You will hear the sentences from the grammar box. Most unstressed vowels in English are pronounced "uh," called the* schwa *sound. Listen to the sentences and underline the schwa sounds.*

Activity A 🎧 Listen to your teacher or the audio. In your notebook, write the sentences that you hear. With your partner, decide if each sentence is true or false.

Activity B **Group Chat Follow-Up** Look at your pie chart. Explain two of the choices you made for your pie chart. Write in your notebook.

I chose "theft" because it's a problem in my neighborhood.

Activity C Listen to your teacher or the audio. You will hear more of Olivia's conversation with the insurance agent. Write the missing words in the blanks.

Olivia: How much does renters insurance cost?

Agent: You _____ about how much your belongings are worth. For example, if you want $30,000 worth of coverage, you _____ about $200 a year. For replacement insurance, you _____ a little more.

Olivia: What's replacement insurance?

Agent: The company will pay you enough money to buy new belongings. Without replacement insurance, the company only _____ what your belongings are worth now. For example, your five-year-old TV may only be worth $50, but if you _____ a new one, you'll spend a lot more.

TASK 2: Analyze an Insurance Policy

With your partner, look at the homeowners insurance policy to see if the following situations are covered. Write *yes* or *no* next to each sentence. When you've finished, compare your answers with the rest of your group.

> plumbing

The Security Plus **Homeowners Policy**	Provides complete coverage for your home in case of fire, lightning, wind and hail, smoke, vandalism, theft, water damage from plumbing, freezing of plumbing, people injured at your home, and people injured by your pets.

_____ **1.** Someone breaks into the house and takes the TV and stereo.

_____ **2.** A bad storm damages the roof.

_no_ **3.** Your cat destroys the new curtains.

_____ **4.** Someone breaks into the garage and sprays paint on the walls.

_____ **5.** Your Aunt Nancy falls down the stairs and breaks her ankle.

_____ **6.** The fruit tree in your backyard freezes and dies.

For each situation that is not covered, explain why in your notebook.

3. The policy doesn't cover damage from pets.

Saving for a Rainy Day

◆ Learn about different kinds of savings plans
◆ Learn about saving and spending in the US

withdrawal

maturity

penalty

term

Is it important to you to save money? How do you save money for the future?

◆ **Reading Tip** When you see symbols like + and * in something you are reading, look for an explanation of what they mean. Before you read this flyer, look for the following symbols: +, *, and **. What do they mean?

Premier National Bank

Account	Minimum Deposit	Term	Interest Rate	Minimum Balance
Regular Savings	$5.00		2.47%	$5.00
CD*	$1,000	3 month +	3.73%	$1,000
		12 month +	4.40%	
		36 month +	4.64%	
		48 month +	4.88%	
Money Market Account**	$2,500		2.97%	$2,500
			3.16%	$10,000
			3.54%	$25,000
			3.82%	$50,000 and above

We offer regular savings accounts; CDs, or certificates of deposit; and money market accounts.

* There is a penalty for withdrawals before the maturity date.
**A total of six withdrawals per month

Talk or Write

1. What is the interest rate for a regular savings account?
2. What is the minimum deposit for a money market account?
3. Does a 3-month CD with $1,000 have a lower or higher interest rate than a money market account of $2,500?
4. Which savings plan has the highest interest rate?

In the US   Planning Ahead

Many people in the US like the idea of retiring early, but studies show that most people are not financially prepared. Early retirement can mean 20 to 30 years of living without working. Government plans, such as Social Security, cannot pay for such long-term retirement. So personal savings plans are necessary. But many people in the US have a lot of debt and save little money. They often use credit for major purchases rather than saving for them. The problem with credit is that people must pay high interest or finance charges on their monthly balance, which makes it difficult to save money.

☛ **Compare Cultures** Think about how people from your home country plan ahead. Compare your home country to the US. Write your ideas in the chart. Share with the class.

	US	Home Country
Savings		
Insurance		
Government Assistance		
Credit		

Vocabulary

Repeat these words after your teacher. Talk about their meanings. Write the words in your notebook. With a partner, write a sentence using each word.

certificate of deposit (CD)

debt

interest rate

money market account

penalty

retire/retirement

Idiom Watch!

save for a rainy day

finance charge

Activity A   With your partner, brainstorm reasons to save. Use an idea map like the one below to write your ideas about things that you would like to save for. Choose three of the following ideas: children, retirement, home, vacation, personal. Add details around the circles. Share your ideas with your group.

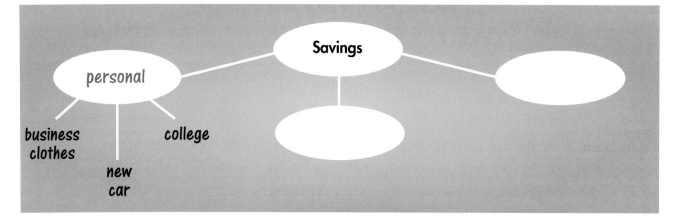

Activity B Practice asking and answering the questions with your partner. One person is the customer, and the other is the bank employee. The bank employee uses the chart on page 54 to answer the questions.

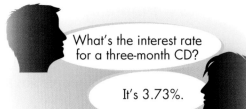

What's the interest rate for a three-month CD?

It's 3.73%.

1. What kinds of savings accounts do you have?
2. What is the minimum deposit for a _____?
3. What's the interest rate for a _____?
4. Can I withdraw money without a penalty?

Activity C Interview four classmates who are not in your group. Take notes on their answers. Share the information with your group.

1. If you received a $2,000 gift, would you save it or spend it?
2. Where would you save it, or how would you spend it?
3. Are you concerned about saving for retirement? Why or why not?
4. Do you think it's OK to pay for large purchases with credit?
5. What kinds of things do you think are a waste of money?

With your group, write sentences about your class.

Most students want to save the money.

Many students want to save for a new car.

waste money
waste of money

Only one person wants to save the money. Three people want to spend it.

 TASK 3: Choose a Savings Account

You have ten thousand dollars ($10,000) to save. Look at the three accounts explained on the flyer. Write answers to the following questions:

1. What would you like to save for?
2. How soon will you need the money?
3. How much will you put into each account?

Decide where to put the money. You can divide it or put it into one account.

Regular Savings	CD	Money Market Account

On the board, write the total amount of money saved by the class ($10,000 × number of students). Make three columns with headings like the ones above. Under each heading, enter the total amount of money deposited by the class. Discuss which choice was the most popular and why.

Do a Survey

Do a survey of your friends or classmates to find out their savings and insurance needs. Follow these steps:

Get Ready

Work with your group. Make a list of eight to ten people that you want to survey about their savings and insurance needs. Include family, friends, or classmates. Make sure each group member is talking to different people. Make a chart like the one to the right.

Number of People Interviewed _____			
Insurance/Savings Account	**Have**	**Don't Have**	**Want**
Homeowners			
Renters			
Auto			
Earthquake			
Flood		✔	✔
Medical			
Dental			
Vision			
Life			
Regular Savings Account			
CD			
Money Market Account			

Do the Work

Talk with eight to ten people. Find out what types of insurance and savings accounts they have, don't have, and want. Put check marks in the correct columns in the chart.

Present

Tally the number of check marks in each column. Share your results with your group. Tell which kinds of savings plans most people have, don't have, and want.

Do you have auto insurance?

Yes. I have to have auto insurance in this state.

Writing Extension Write a paragraph about the kinds of insurance many people have and the kinds few people have. Explain the results.

🖥 Technology Extra

Search the Web for information on affordable insurance. Use the key words "renters insurance," "homeowners insurance," "health insurance," "medical insurance," "dental insurance," and "vision insurance."

Making Ends Meet

◆ **Vocabulary** Shopping words
◆ **Language** Superlative adjectives • *Used to*
◆ **Pronunciation** Stress on superlative adjectives • Reductions
◆ **Culture** Second-hand shopping

Which things are important to you when you buy something? Quality? Price? Warranty?

Gail and Trevor Granville and their daughter, Tremaine, need to buy some new items, but they don't have a lot of money. They are looking for good quality at bargain prices.

Think and Talk

1. Describe what you see in the picture.
2. What do you think each of the Granvilles wants to buy?
3. Do you think a garage sale is a good place for them to shop?
4. Where do you shop for bargains?

What's Your Opinion? Is it OK to buy things that you want instead of things that you need? When is it OK? When is it not OK?

Gather Your Thoughts

Discuss these questions with your partner. Take notes in the chart.

> I always want a warranty when I buy a machine.

Questions	Answers
When do you think it's important to have a warranty?	*expensive items; machines*
Did you ever buy something defective? What happened?	
What kinds of things do stores guarantee?	
Did you ever exchange an item? What item?	
Did you ever ask for a refund? What happened?	
Do you care more about quality or price?	
What would you buy that wasn't in perfect condition?	

Vocabulary

Repeat these words after your teacher. Talk about their meanings. Write the words in your notebook. With a partner, write a sentence using each word.

> condition
> defective
> quality
> second-hand
> warranty

> exchange
> guarantee
> refund

Idiom Watch!

make ends meet

Vocabulary Plus

The words *exchange, guarantee,* and *refund* can be nouns or verbs.
refund = noun or verb
re**fund** = verb

What's the Problem?

Comparison shopping is important for saving money. What makes it difficult for people to do comparison shopping? Think or talk with a partner. Tell your group your ideas.

Setting Goals

Shopping is an important part of everyone's life. Which of the following goals are most important to you? Rank them from 1 (most important) to 6.

_____ **a.** describe items that I want to return

_____ **b.** understand catalog descriptions

_____ **c.** interpret newspaper ads

_____ **d.** ask for information about products

_____ **e.** describe items that I want to sell

_____ **f.** another goal: _____

Which was the most important goal for your class? Tally your answers.
Talk about your most important goals.

Getting the Most for Your Money

◆ Identify and describe product features
◆ Use superlatives

| compact |
| extended |
| handle |
| limited |

Have you ever had a new machine break down? Were you able to return it? Describe what happened.

◆ **Reading Tip** When you compare items, you need to look carefully at their specific features. As you read the descriptions of the printers, look for information about the speed, price, quality, warranty, and size of each one.

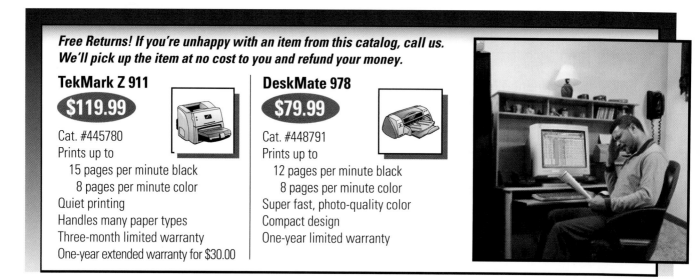

Free Returns! *If you're unhappy with an item from this catalog, call us. We'll pick up the item at no cost to you and refund your money.*

TekMark Z 911

$119.99

Cat. #445780
Prints up to
  15 pages per minute black
  8 pages per minute color
Quiet printing
Handles many paper types
Three-month limited warranty
One-year extended warranty for $30.00

DeskMate 978

$79.99

Cat. #448791
Prints up to
  12 pages per minute black
  8 pages per minute color
Super fast, photo-quality color
Compact design
One-year limited warranty

Trevor and Gail have a small home office for their air-conditioning business. Trevor needs to order a new printer.

Idiom Watch!
break down
get the most for your money

Talk or Write

1. Which printer is faster?
2. Which printer is probably bigger?
3. Which one has the best warranty?
4. Which one do you think Trevor should buy? Why?

Group Chat

Make two charts like the ones below. Ask your group members this question: "What is your most _____ item?" Write answers in the charts.

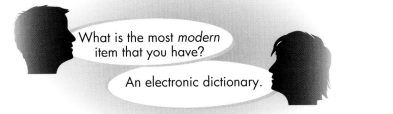

What is the most *modern* item that you have?

An electronic dictionary.

What is the most _____ item that you have?

Name	compact	durable	efficient	lightweight

Name	modern	portable	powerful	useful

Vocabulary

Repeat these words after your teacher. Talk about their meanings. Write the words in your notebook. With a partner, write a sentence using each word.

compact

durable

efficient

lightweight

modern

portable

powerful

useful

Grammar Talk: Superlative Adjectives

I want the high**est** quality video camera that you sell.

I'm looking for the **most** compact cell phone that you have.

I want the remote control that is the easi**est** to use.

The tape recorder had the **best** warranty that I could find.

That store has the **worst** service in town.

When you use a superlative, how many things are you comparing?
How do you form the superlative for one- and two-syllable adjectives
*and adjectives that end in **y**? With your class, make a list of rules.*
What are the superlative forms for good *and* bad?

When you compare only two things, you use comparative adjectives.
My computer at work is fast**er** than my computer at home.
My new phone is **more** compact than my old phone.

Pronunciation Target • Stress on Superlative Adjectives

🎧 *Listen to your teacher or the audio. You will hear the sentences in the grammar box. Notice that the superlative adjectives are stressed.*

Activity A **Group Chat Follow-Up** Look at the charts from your Group Chat. Write sentences in your notebook using each adjective from the charts.

The most modern item that I have is my electronic dictionary.

Activity B Look at the charts from your Group Chat. Decide which items are the most useful, the most efficient, the easiest to use, the hardest to use, and the least durable. Tell your partner your ideas. Practice stressing the superlative adjectives.

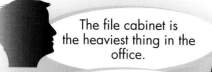

Cell phones are the most useful items on the charts because you can use them anywhere.

Maybe, but they aren't the most efficient because they don't always work.

Activity C Trevor is calling the office supply company to order his new printer. He is speaking to a salesperson named Fernando. Write their conversation and practice it with your partner.

Activity D Below is a list of some of the things in Trevor's office. Talk about these items using the superlative.

The file cabinet is the heaviest thing in the office.

The computer is the most important because his accounts are on it.

Answering machine
size, 8″ x 10″; weight, 5 lbs.; price, $120; age, 6 years old; uses a cassette tape for recording messages.

Computer
size, 16″ x 24″ with a 15″ monitor; weight, 30 lbs.; price, $2,000; 4 years old; Trevor uses it to organize all of his accounts.

File cabinet
size, 5′ x 2′ x 3′; weight, 200 lbs.; price, $150; 10 years old; Trevor keeps important papers in it, but it isn't very well-organized.

Fax machine
18″ x 24″; weight, 20 lbs.; price, $200; 3 years old; Trevor uses it every day to send out and receive orders.

TASK 1: Find the Best Deal

Look at the list of printing calculators, their speed, prices, sizes, and lengths of warranty. Rank the items, with the best deal first. Explain your choice to the class.

Q5-2761A	Prints 4.5 lines per second	$159.99	9″ x 12″	lifetime warranty
CS0-265B	Prints 3 lines per second	$69.99	10″ x 13″	3-year warranty
MP-275B	Prints 3.6 lines per second	$89.99	7″ x 9″	5-year warranty
P1-1357L	Prints 2.4 lines per second	$39.99	10″ x 8″	1-month warranty

Second-Hand Rose

- Learn about second-hand shopping
- Talk about the past with *used to*

Have you ever bought anything second-hand? What was it? Describe your experience.

- **Listening Tip** When you listen to a radio announcement, it is helpful to think about who the announcement is for. Listen to your teacher or the audio. What age group do you think this radio ad is trying to appeal to? You can read the words on page 119.

appeal

brand-name

label

wildest

Idiom Watch!

nearly new

treat yourself

Tremaine's eighth-grade class is having a party. She doesn't want to wear an old dress, and Gail doesn't think they can afford to buy a new one. She tells Tremaine about a radio ad that she heard.

Talk or Write

1. What kind of store is Second-Hand Rose?
2. What's the difference between shopping at a department store and shopping at Second-Hand Rose?
3. On which days is the store closed?
4. What time does the store close?

Partner Chat   Make a chart like this one. Ask your partner the questions. Write the answers in the correct column.

	Where do you shop?	Where did you use to shop?
Clothes	department stores	dress shops
Furniture		
Equipment		

Grammar Talk: *Used to*

Tremaine's dress **used to** fit.

This sweater **used to** be pretty, but now it's faded.

I **used to** shop every weekend.

Did you **use to** shop there?

What does used to *mean? What is the form of the verb after* used to? *In the fourth sentence, why is* use to *in simple form?*

Look at the following sentence. Can you change threw away *to* used to throw away?

Tremaine threw away her ripped jeans yesterday.

What's the difference between the simple past and used to?

Vocabulary

Repeat these words after your teacher. Talk about their meanings. Write the words in your notebook. With a partner, write a sentence using each word.

faded

ripped

scratched

stained

defect

flaw

rip

scratch

equipment

Pronunciation Target • Reductions

🎧 *Listen to your teacher or the audio. You will hear sentences from the grammar box. Notice that the vowel sound in* to *is reduced to* uh, *the schwa sound. Practice saying the sentences with a partner.*

Activity A **Partner Chat Follow-Up** Use the ideas from your Partner Chat to write sentences in your notebook. Write about where you both used to shop.

I used to buy my clothes at a dress shop. Now I buy them at a department store.

Te Chi used to buy food on the street, but they don't sell food on the street here.

Activity B Think about places where you used to shop and things that you used to buy in your home country or when you were younger. Tell your group what you used to do and why you don't do it anymore. After everyone has spoken, write as many sentences as you can about your group members. Write some of your sentences on the board.

> When I was a kid, I used to buy a lot of candy, but now I don't. It's not good for me.

Gideon used to buy a lot of candy, but he doesn't eat candy anymore.

Grammar Talk: *One/Ones*

I'm going to buy that shirt. This **one** has a flaw.

These shoes are stained. I need some new **ones.**

Notice that shirt *is not repeated in the second sentence. It is replaced with* one. *Plural nouns are replaced with* ones.

Activity C 🎧 Listen to your teacher or the audio. Then, with your class, brainstorm the names of clothing items and accessories. Use the words in the vocabulary box on page 64 to describe what's wrong with the items. Practice returning or exchanging the items.

TASK 2: Describe Items for Sale

Draw or cut out a picture of a piece of clothing that you want to sell. Write a description. Explain any defects, tell about the history of the item, and give it a price. Try to convince your group members to buy it.

This coat will keep you warm during the cold winters. It's in perfect condition, with no rips or stains. There's a small scratch on one of the buttons. The hood will keep the rain or snow off of your head. It looks like new, and I only wore it once on a short trip to the mountains. Unfortunately, I used to be thinner than I am now, and I can't wear it anymore. A bargain for you at $20.00!

Bargain Hunting

◆ Find bargains in the newspaper
◆ Learn about second-hand shopping in the US

attachment
cf (cubic feet)
obo (or best offer)
w/ (with)

Have you ever read the classified ads? What kind of ads did you read?

◆ **Reading Tip** When you read classified ads, you need to understand many abbreviations. Find the abbreviations in the following classified ad section. Discuss what they mean.

Idiom Watch!
bargain hunting
early bird

Furniture

SOFA tan, 1 yr-old, xlnt cond
value $1400, sell $500 555-4692

CRNR DESK 70x70x28
$150 obo 555-5574

Appliances

FRIDGE, ice maker
18 cf, white, $100 555-4300

VACUUM CLEANER w/attachments
like new $45 555-1317

Garage Sale

NO EARLY BIRDS!
7 am - 1 pm • Saturday and Sunday
Lots of furniture, antiques, jewelry.

Moving Sale

Saturday Only
7am – 3pm, 117 Main St.
toys, clothing, furniture, washer/dryer

We need a new cabinet for all those CDs you bought!

Trevor didn't find a printer at the garage sale, but he did find a collection of jazz CDs that was a great deal. The CDs have been on the coffee table ever since the garage sale.

Talk or Write Scan the ads for the answers to these questions.

1. How much is the sofa?
2. Do you have to pay $150 if you want to buy the desk?
3. How big is the refrigerator?
4. Where might Trevor and Gail find a CD cabinet?

Now go back and read carefully to check your answers.

In the US Second-Hand Shopping

In the US there are many kinds of places to buy and sell second-hand items. Thrift stores sell clothing and items that people give away. Second-hand clothing stores sell used clothing and accessories that have been chosen carefully. Sometimes these stores sell other items on *consignment*. This means that people bring in items they want to sell. If the items are sold, the store receives a percentage of the price. A pawn shop is another place to buy used items. People sell valuable items, such as jewelry and musical instruments, to pawn-shop owners. The pawn shop sells the items back to the owner or to other customers for a higher price.

One popular place to buy and sell used items is a garage sale or sidewalk sale. Some people buy used items because they need to save money. Other people just like to shop at garage sales and find bargains. Many people in the US move frequently. When they move, they often sell items that they no longer want. Sometimes neighborhoods have group garage sales. Everyone on the block sells items on the same day. It's OK to bargain for a cheaper price at a garage sale.

Vocabulary

Repeat these words after your teacher. Talk about their meanings. Write the words in your notebook. With a partner, write a sentence using each word.

- aquarium
- blender
- crib
- hamper
- nightstand
- recliner
- stroller

give away

☞ Compare Cultures

Does your home country have these kinds of stores and sales? Fill in the chart by putting a check under yes or no.

US	Your Home Country	
	yes	no
thrift stores		
second-hand stores		
consignment shops		
pawn shops		
garage sales		

Activity A Make a list of things you have bought or would buy second-hand and things you wouldn't. Compare your lists in a small group and explain reasons for your choices.

Activity B   As a class, make a list of things that could be sold at a garage sale. Put them under the headings *Living Room, Bedroom, Kitchen,* and *Garage*. With your partner, describe the items that you would like to buy. Be specific about the size, color, and condition of the item you are looking for.

> I want a small, lightweight stroller for my baby. It has to be in perfect condition.

> I want a lawn mower that works. I don't care what it looks like.

Activity C   Practice this conversation with your partner. Then write a new conversation, using a different item that you would like to sell at a garage sale. Try to convince your partner to buy the item.

Katie: How old is this recliner?

Maddy: It's three years old, but we didn't use it very much.

Katie: How much do you want for it?

Maddy: Well, I paid $800, but I'll sell it for $200.

Katie: I saw an ad for a cheaper one. Would you take $100?

Maddy: How about $150? This is really durable, and it's in excellent condition.

Katie: Well, I guess that's OK.

TASK 3: Ask for Information about Items for Sale

Look at the list of items for sale from a classified ad section.

stroller	recliner
crib	camera
nightstand	aquarium
hamper	blender
bicycle	tennis racket

Choose three items you might want to buy and a price that you would pay. What would you need to know about the items? Write questions that you would ask if you called about the item.

blender $5 – $10

• How old is it?

• How big is it?

• How many speeds does it have?

• Does it chop ice?

• What color is it?

• Does it work well?

Classroom "Garage Sale"

Have a classroom garage sale. Follow these steps:

Get Ready

Draw or cut out pictures of five items that you would like to sell. If possible, choose items that you actually have at home and would like to sell. Write information about the item on an index card like the one at the right. In your description, use adjectives and give other information about the item.

Name:
How Old:
Price:
Description:

Do the Work

Divide the class into "buyers" and "sellers." The sellers spread their pictures out on their desks or tables. The buyers walk around deciding what they want to buy. The sellers try to convince the buyers to choose their items. When an agreement is reached, the buyer takes the picture. After 15 minutes, the sellers put away the unsold items. Buyers become sellers, and the new sellers display their items. Repeat the process for 15 more minutes.

Present

Tell the class which items you sold, which items you couldn't sell, and why.

Writing Extension Write a paragraph about what you chose to buy. Explain why you bought the items.

🖥 Technology Extra

Search a web site that sells second-hand items. Try search terms like "used clothing," "used appliances," and "second-hand furniture." Look for an item that you are interested in buying. Report back to the class on what you find. Discuss the advantages and disadvantages of purchasing on the Internet.

Facing Problems Head On

Dealing with Abuse

Work/School 1
Home 2
Community 3

- ◆ **Vocabulary** Words about abuse and support
- ◆ **Language** Gerunds as subjects and objects • Present perfect
- ◆ **Pronunciation** Reduction of -*ing* • Disappearing initial *h*
- ◆ **Culture** Disciplining children

What are some reasons people go to a medical clinic?

Leticia Medina is a nurse in a medical clinic. She often sees the results of violence, neglect, and abuse. Lately, however, these problems have affected people that she knows. She wants to learn more about drug abuse and child abuse and how to help people who struggle with these problems.

Think and Talk

1. What do you see in the picture?
2. What kinds of problems do you think the patients have?
3. Do you think that these problems are common? Explain.
4. Why do you think people have these problems?

What's Your Opinion? Which of the following causes more problems in society: tobacco, alcohol, or illegal drugs? Explain your answer.

Gather Your Thoughts

Work with a partner. Talk about each of these topics. Take notes in the chart.

What do you know about alcoholism?

It's difficult to recover.

Drug Abuse	Alcoholism	Child Abuse
	difficult to recover	

What's the Problem?

Most people don't know what to do or where to go for help when someone they know is abusive or addicted to drugs or alcohol. What are some things people can do in these situations? Think or talk with a partner.

Setting Goals

Drug abuse and violence are very common in today's society, so it is important for people to be informed about them. Which of the following goals is most important to you? Rank them from 1 (most important) to 6.

_____ **a.** describe symptoms of drug abuse

_____ **b.** explain my ideas about disciplining children

_____ **c.** understand laws about child abuse

_____ **d.** write a convincing argument about drug or alcohol laws

_____ **e.** be able to make a telephone call to a government agency

_____ **f.** another goal: _____

Which was the most important goal for your class? Tally your answers. Talk about your most important goals.

Vocabulary

Repeat these words after your teacher. Talk about their meanings. Write the words in your notebook. With a partner, write a sentence using each word.

abuse/abusive

addict/addicted

alcoholic/alcoholism

anonymous

recover

support

symptom

Idiom Watch!
face head on

Vocabulary Plus
noun = [a buse]
verb = [a buze]

Laying Down the Law

◆ Learn about drug and alcohol laws
◆ Use gerunds

randomly
refer
terminate
test positive
third party

What kinds of occupations often require drug tests?

◆ **Reading Tip** To better understand what you read, think about what you already know about the topic before you start reading. This is a memo about the new drug-testing policy at Leticia's clinic. Before you read, discuss with your class what you know about drug testing.

To: All Employees
From: Management
Re: Drug Testing Policy

The drug-testing program that we talked about in our last meeting will begin next week. The purpose of our new drug-testing program is to increase workplace safety.

We will test employees before they are hired, after an accident, when drug use is suspected, and randomly.

Employees will be chosen for random testing by the computer system, using ID numbers.

An employee who tests positive will be tested again.

We will not share the results of a drug test with any other employee or any third party.

If we find that the employee's positive drug test is caused by drug abuse, we will refer the employee to a drug treatment program at the employee's expense. Employees who do not complete the program will be terminated.

Idiom Watch!
lay down the law

Talk or Write
1. Why is the clinic giving drug tests?
2. When will employees be tested?
3. What will happen to employees who test positive?

What's Your Opinion? Would you be offended if your employer decided to give you a drug test? Why or why not?

Class Chat Make a chart like the one below. Discuss the questions with your class. Write several answers to every question.

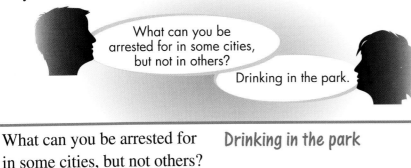

What can you be arrested for in some cities, but not others?	*Drinking in the park*
What can you receive a jail sentence for?	
What is not allowed in school?	
Where is smoking prohibited in your state?	

Vocabulary

Repeat these words after your teacher. Talk about their meanings. Write the words in your notebook. With a partner, write a sentence using each word.

allow

arrest

prohibit

fine

sentence

substance

illegal

Grammar Talk: Gerunds as Subjects and Objects

Smoking at work is prohibited in some states.

She's worried about **going** to jail.

You could receive a fine for **smoking** marijuana.

The words that end in -ing *look like verbs, but they are nouns. They are called gerunds. Which ones are subjects and which ones are objects? Notice that a gerund is used after* for *and* about.

Pronunciation Target • Reduction of *-ing*

🎧 *Listen to your teacher or the audio. You will hear the sentences in the grammar box. Notice that the* -ing *sound is reduced to "en" because it is not stressed. This sometimes makes it difficult to hear the gerund. Practice saying each sentence with a partner.*

Activity A **Class Chat Follow-Up** Look at the Class Chat chart. Choose one answer for each question and write it in your notebook. Use a gerund.

In some cities, you can be arrested for drinking in the park.

Activity B   With your group, write sentences about your classroom. Use *prohibited, allowed,* or *not allowed.* Use a gerund subject.

Using dictionaries is not allowed during tests.
_____

Activity C 🎧 Listen to your teacher or the audio. You will hear sentences about drugs and alcohol. Write them in your notebook. Listen for the gerund. Check the sentences with your class. Then read them with your partner.

Activity D   Discuss these questions with your group. Take notes.

1. What problems do drugs and alcohol cause in your home country? How do they compare to problems in the US?
2. How does the government handle drug use in your home country?
3. What do you think the US government should do about drugs and alcohol?
4. Does your home country have a drinking age limit? What is it? Do you think it's appropriate?
5. What do you think about the drinking age limits in the US?
6. What are other laws about alcohol use in this country?

Put the headings below on the board. Use your notes to write some ideas under each heading. Have a class discussion.

Drug and Alcohol Problems   **Government Solutions**   **Your Solutions**

TASK 1: Write a Convincing Argument

With your partner, choose to agree or disagree with one of these statements:

- All employers should be able to randomly drug test their employees.
- Marijuana should be legal.
- Smoking should not be allowed in public.
- The drinking age should be 18.

- If people use drugs, they should go to jail.
- Alcohol should not be allowed at sporting events.
- Drug addicts should go to treatment centers, not to jail.

Write an argument explaining your opinion. Include an example to make your opinion convincing. Specific examples are more convincing. Compare the two arguments to the right.

Share your argument with another pair. Try to convince them that you are right. Talk to two more pairs. When everyone finishes, decide which pair was the most convincing and tell why.

Teenagers drink anyway, so why not make it legal? [weak]

In my home country, teenagers are allowed to drink alcohol. Drinking wasn't exciting to us because it wasn't prohibited. I didn't know many people who abused alcohol. [more convincing]

Protecting Children

◆ Understand laws about child abuse
◆ Learn about attitudes toward corporal punishment

authority
discipline
harm
neglect

Have you ever been shocked by the way that someone was treating a child?

◆ **Reading Tip** Setting a purpose for reading can help you understand. The purpose for reading this information is to find out when you must report child abuse.

Child Abuse

Who is required to report?
Anyone who has reason to believe that a child has been abused or neglected is required to report it to the authorities.

What must I report?
You must report suspected abuse or neglect of a child. Abuse means mental or emotional injury to a child, physical injury (not including accidents or normal discipline by a parent), or sexual behavior that harms a child. An example of neglect is leaving a child in a situation where the child could be harmed.

What if I am not sure that the child is really being abused?
The law does not require you to be completely sure that a child has been abused or neglected. It requires only that you have a reason to suspect that a child is being abused.

What can happen if I don't make a report?
If you don't make a report of suspected child abuse, you could receive a fine of up to $2,000 or go to jail for 180 days, or both. People who are licensed to work with children may also lose their certificate or license if they don't report suspected child abuse.

Leticia suspects that her neighbor is abusing her child, but she doesn't know if she should get involved.

Talk or Write
1. What is the difference between abuse and neglect?
2. What are some behaviors you think would be neglect rather than abuse?
3. If a teacher suspects child abuse but doesn't report it, what can happen?

In the US   Disciplining Children

Corporal punishment, such as hitting or spanking, is one form of disciplining children. People in the US have strong feelings about it. Some people believe that corporal punishment may harm children. Others believe that corporal punishment is sometimes necessary. Some parents use spanking for discipline, but few use it as the most important form. Most parents prefer talking to children, or using *time out,* where children are made to sit quietly. Parents often punish older children by *grounding* them—not allowing them to leave home except to go to school.

About half of the states in the US have laws that forbid corporal punishment in schools. Where it is permitted, it is often not done. However, some people believe that it is a good way to control students' behavior. Corporal punishment in schools is called *paddling* because students are hit with a flat wooden paddle. Schools that use paddling must have a policy defining how it may be used. The policy explains what the paddle is made of and how many times the student may be hit.

☛ **Compare Cultures**   Are attitudes toward disciplining children different in your home country than they are in the US? How? Write your ideas in circles like the ones below. Discuss with your group.

Home Country
Spanking kids in school is OK.

US
Spanking kids in most schools is not OK.

Activity A   As a class, make a list of behaviors that children and teenagers are often punished for. Make another list of ways that children are disciplined. Talk to your partner about your ideas on using corporal punishment to discipline children in school and at home.

I think it's OK to spank children if they do something dangerous.

It's important not to hit a child when you're angry.

Vocabulary

Repeat these words after your teacher. Talk about their meanings. Write the words in your notebook. With a partner, write a sentence using each word.

beat

forbid

ground

harm

permit

slap

spank

corporal punishment

discipline

neglect

Idiom Watch!
get involved

Vocabulary Plus
The words *discipline* and *neglect* are nouns and verbs.

Activity B   In your group, use the following verbs in the gerund form. Think of several sentences for each word.

abuse   get involved   neglect   spank

beat   ground   slap

> Slapping a child can teach a child to slap other kids.

> She was punished for slapping her brother.

Activity C   With your partner, discuss the following actions. Make two columns in your notebook with the headings *Abuse-Neglect* and *Acceptable Behavior*. Write the actions in the appropriate column.

- slap a child in the face several times
- neglect a child's health needs
- lock a child in the closet for discipline
- not help a child with homework

- discipline a child by taking away TV time
- slap a child's hand
- spank a child with a belt
- beat a child

Activity D   Read the brochure on page 75 again. With your partner, decide which of the following situations are examples of abuse or neglect. Write *yes* next to those sentences. Talk about the other sentences with your group. Do you think the parents are right or wrong in these situations?

_____   **1.** A mother spanks her child for breaking a dish.

_____   **2.** A father leaves his 5-year-old son at a playground while he goes to the bank.

_____   **3.** A child is walking with his dad, and the child falls and gets hurt.

_____   **4.** Parents go on vacation and leave their 10-year-old at home alone.

_____   **5.** A mother sends her child to bed without dinner because he came home dirty.

_____   **6.** A mother leaves her young child in a car while she goes grocery shopping.

_____   **7.** The parents travel in the front of a pickup truck with two children sitting between them and a baby sitting on the mother's lap.

TASK 2: Write a Handout about Discipline

Imagine that you have been asked to meet with a group of new parents. Work with your group to develop a handout about how to discipline children.

Take notes about these ideas before you design your handout: What is appropriate discipline? What is inappropriate? Should people get involved when they suspect child abuse? What should they do?

Practice meeting with the "new parents." Your classmates are the parents. Share your handout with the class.

A Helping Hand

◆ Learn about getting support
◆ Use the present perfect

Where can people go for help with drug and alcohol problems?

◆ **Listening Tip** 🎧 When you take notes on something you listen to, listen the first time without writing. When you listen the second time, write down important words. This ad begins with a list of questions. Take notes on the questions. You can read the words on page 119.

> crave
>
> dignity
>
> outpatient
>
> privacy
>
> residential

Idiom Watch!
helping hand

When Leticia sees an ad for a treatment center on television, she realizes that the treatment center might be able to give her advice about helping her neighbor.

Talk or Write

Try to remember the main ideas of the questions. Using your notes, write questions like the ones in the ad. Don't worry about the exact words. There are seven questions in the ad. Write as many as you can remember.

Group Chat Use the words in the chart below to talk to your group about someone you have known. In the right column, explain what the person did.

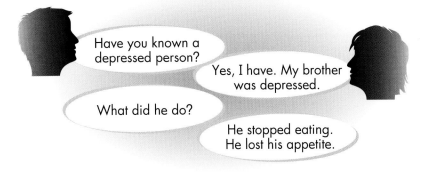

Vocabulary

Repeat these words after your teacher. Talk about their meanings. Write the words in your notebook. With a partner, write a sentence using each word.

appetite
depression
enthusiasm

aggressive
depressed
enthusiastic
irrational

Have you known a/an _____ person?	What did the person do?
depressed	He stopped eating.
aggressive	
enthusiastic	
irrational	

Grammar Talk: Present Perfect

Present Perfect
He **has been arrested** three times.
I **have seen** people drinking in the park.
She **has lost** her enthusiasm for exercise.
Has she ever **missed** work because of depression?

Simple Past
He **was arrested** yesterday.
I **saw** people drinking in the park last weekend.

The present perfect uses a helping verb and a main verb. Underline the helping verb in each sentence. What is the form of the main verb? In the fourth sentence, what does the word ever *mean?*

The sentences listed under "Simple Past" cannot be changed to present perfect. How are they different from the sentences listed under "Present Perfect"? With your teacher, write a rule about the difference between the present perfect and the simple past.

Activity A **Group Chat Follow-Up** Look at the chart from your Group Chat. Use the information to write sentences in your notebook.

My brother was depressed. He didn't eat all day.

Pronunciation Target • Disappearing Initial *h*

🎧 *Listen to your teacher or the audio. Focus on the words that begin with* h.

Where **have** you been all day?
He has been aggressive lately.
They arrested **him** for driving too fast.

Notice that the h *often disappears in spoken English. Which one of the* h *sounds could you hear clearly? When a word is stressed, the* h *is pronounced clearly.*

Is the h *pronounced clearly in the following sentence? Why?*
The treatment center **helped** the woman.

Activity B Imagine that someone has a problem with drugs or alcohol. Tell your group why you think the person has a problem. Use the present perfect and the following time expressions in your conversation.

a few times	never	this week
many times	this month	this year

He has been late to work many times.

He has come to work a few times with very red eyes.

Activity C Change these sentences into the present perfect. Change the time expression if necessary. Read the sentences to your partner. Listen to your partner's advice.

1. My friend got drunk three times this month.
2. My teenager came home late every night last week.
3. My son's room smelled like tobacco a few times.
4. My daughter didn't eat anything all day.
5. My niece was arrested twice for selling drugs.

My teenager has come home late every night this week.

Take away his telephone for a week.

TASK 3: Write and Practice a Call to a Hotline

People call hotlines to talk about serious problems. The calls are anonymous.

With a partner, write a call to a hotline. The hotline operator asks questions, and the caller answers. Then the operator gives advice. Create your own situation or use Leticia's. Practice in pairs. Share with two other pairs.

Make a Booklet

Make a booklet about drug abuse, alcohol abuse, and child abuse. Follow these steps:

Get Ready

With your group, collect information about the topics below. Divide the research among your group members. You can use information from this unit. You can also look in the phone book or on the Internet, or go to a local library, hospital, or police station. Organize the information that your group has gathered under the correct headings.

- Alcohol Laws
- Drug Laws
- Drug Testing
- Drug Abuse Symptoms
- Drug and Alcohol Treatment Centers
- Child Abuse Laws
- Corporal Punishment

Do the Work

Make a booklet with one page about each of the topics. If possible, include phone numbers and other important information about your community. Draw or cut out pictures to illustrate your work.

Present

Share your booklet with other groups. Display the booklets, if possible, for other classes as well.

Writing Extension   Write a paragraph about why you think people use drugs and alcohol. Include at least one example.

🖉💻 Technology Extra

Use the Internet to get more information about hotlines and local support groups. Use the search terms "substance abuse hotlines," "substance abuse treatment centers," "substance abuse support," "Alcoholics Anonymous," "Al-Anon," and "Child Protective Services."

Pitching In

Getting Involved

Home Community Work/School
  1   2   3

◆ **Vocabulary** Community involvement words

◆ **Language** Verbs followed by gerunds • Present perfect with *for* and *since*

◆ **Pronunciation** Diphthongs • Stress on adjectives

◆ **Culture** Processes for change

> **Do you know of a place that has problems like the ones that you see in this picture?**

Marlene and her daughter, Jenny, are talking to their neighbors at a park near their homes. They both enjoy being involved in their community. They know that they can help improve things in their neighborhood.

Think and Talk

1. What do you see in the photograph?
2. What do you think Marlene and Jenny are talking about to their neighbors?
3. What can they do to create change in their neighborhood?
4. What can you do to get involved in your community?

What's Your Opinion? If you saw people throwing trash on the ground, would you ask them to pick it up? Explain your answer.

Gather Your Thoughts
In small groups, discuss this question: What events would you like to see happen in your school, neighborhood, or city? Write your ideas in a chart like the one below.

School	Neighborhood	City
international fair		

Look at the ideas in your chart. Discuss how you could help at each event.

I could bring traditional clothing from Korea for the culture fair.

I could serve food at the food bank.

What's the Problem?
Many people would like to help in their communities, but for different reasons, they don't. What prevents people from helping? Discuss your ideas with your partner.

Setting Goals
When people care about their neighborhoods and community, they often want to help make changes. Which of the following goals is most important to you? Rank them from 1 (most important) to 6.

_____ **a.** ask for help with a project

_____ **b.** be able to speak up at a meeting

_____ **c.** learn how to write a petition to change something

_____ **d.** plan a project and describe it in detail

_____ **e.** describe personal qualities you could use on a resume

_____ **f.** another goal: _____

Which was the most important goal for your class? Tally your answers. Talk about your most important goals.

Vocabulary
Repeat these words after your teacher. Talk about their meanings. Write the words in your notebook. With a partner, write a sentence using each word.

block party
carnival
committee
fair
food bank
fund-raiser
mural
parade

Idiom Watch!
pitch in

personal qualities
petition

Get the Ball Rolling

- ◆ Learn how to organize events
- ◆ Use verbs followed by gerunds

Have you ever helped organize an activity with family or friends? Explain.

◆ **Listening Tip** 🎧 Listening for specific information can help you focus on important details. Listen to the conversation. Why is Marlene telling Jenny her plan? You can read the words on page 120.

Idiom Watch!

get the ball rolling

give someone a hand

Marlene likes to take walks in the park near her house. Lately she has noticed a lot of trash in the park, and she wants to do something about it. She is talking to Jenny about her plan.

Talk or Write
1. What does Marlene want to do?
2. What does she have to do to get started?
3. Why isn't Jenny convinced at first?
4. How is Jenny going to help?

Group Chat   Talk about activities, events, or projects that you like doing around your house or in your neighborhood. Write the names of the people in your group in a chart like this one. Write what they like to do. Talk to your group about the events or projects in your chart.

What's your name?	What kinds of projects do you like doing?
Gerardo	working in the backyard

Vocabulary

Repeat these words after your teacher. Talk about their meanings. Write the words in your notebook. With a partner, write a sentence using each word.

- appreciate
- avoid
- consider
- mind
- recommend
- request
- suggest
- volunteer

Grammar Talk: Verbs Followed by Gerunds

Jenny **doesn't mind** help**ing** with family projects.

She **suggested** call**ing** them.

We **finished** remov**ing** the graffiti yesterday.

She **recommended** go**ing** to the meetings.

I **avoid** work**ing** with my brother.

He **appreciated** gett**ing** help.

Marlene **stopped** work**ing** at age 62.

They **considered** paint**ing** a mural.

Look at the verb that comes before the gerund in each sentence. These verbs cannot be followed by the infinitive or simple form.

Vocabulary Plus

Request and *volunteer* can be used as nouns or verbs.

Activity A   In your group, make suggestions or recommendations for planning a big event. Use gerunds after *suggest* and *recommend*.

When you finish, make a class list of recommendations for people who want to organize events. What do you need to do first?

I suggest making a list.

I recommend calling your friends immediately.

Activity B   **Group Chat Follow-Up** Look at the chart from your Group Chat. Number the projects from the easiest to the most difficult. Number 1 is the easiest. Write about the first three projects. Use complete sentences.

Gerardo likes working in the backyard.

Pronunciation Target • Diphthongs

🎧 *Listen to your teacher or the audio. Repeat these words.*

en<u>joy</u>   **n<u>ow</u>**
av<u>oi</u>d   ab<u>ou</u>t

In English, some vowel sounds are two sounds that are pronounced together. With your group, write the words enjoy *and* now, *in a chart like this. In each column, write as many words as you can that have the same vowel sound. See which group has the most words.*

Activity C   Your group is going to have a party. It can be a birthday party, a holiday party, or any other celebration. Make a list of tasks that people can do to help with your party. Divide the tasks among the group members. Walk around the class asking classmates for help. Use the following requests and answers.

> Would you consider singing at my son's graduation party?
>
> I'd be happy to.
>
> I'm sorry, but I only sing in the shower.

Requests

Would you consider _____?
Would you mind _____?

Answers

Sure. No problem.   I'd be happy to.
I'd like to, but _____.   I'm sorry, but _____.

If your classmates agree to help you, thank them like this: "I really appreciate your helping me." Write down the names of the people that will help and what they will do. Report back to your group.

TASK 1: Plan a Project

Choose an event you would like to have in your neighborhood or a household project that you want help with. Make a chart like this one to plan your event or project.

Project/Event	
Location	
Materials	
Expenses	
Number of Helpers	
Tasks	

Fill in the chart with the details of your project. When you are finished, share your plan with your group and other groups.

Sign on the Dotted Line

◆ Make polite requests
◆ Learn about processes for change in the US

Has anyone ever asked you to sign a petition? What was it for?

allow
limit
posted
residents

◆ **Reading Tip** If you want to get the general idea of what something is about, it's a good idea to read it quickly. This is called *skimming*. Skim the paragraph to find out what Marlene wants to change.

Parking Petition

Last year a new hospital was built in our neighborhood. People have been parking on the street because the hospital charges for parking. It is difficult for local residents to find parking in front of their homes. We would like signs posted that limit visitor parking to two hours. We would also like parking permits that allow unlimited parking for residents.

	Print Name	Signature	Address	Telephone
1.	Marlene Cohen	Marlene Cohen	985 Oak St.	(310) 555 - 2987
2.	Jay Brubaker	Jay Brubaker	983 Oak St.	(310) 555 - 9007
3.	Jenny Levits	Jenny Levits	978 Oak St.	(310) 555 - 1024
4.				

Talk or Write

1. Why don't some people park at the hospital?
2. Why do Marlene and her neighbors want two-hour parking limits?
3. How many hours will residents be able to park?
4. Where do you think Marlene will take the petition?

Idiom Watch!

sign on the dotted line

In the US   Speaking Out

In the US, there are many ways for people to change situations. Sometimes, a phone call to complain or report a dangerous situation is enough. Sometimes people start the change process with a petition. People do this at schools, in their communities, and at the state and federal levels. People can express their opinions or influence decision making in this way.

Someone who is not happy with something at a school can talk about the issue or present a petition to a school administrator, at a PTA (Parent and Teacher Association) meeting, or at a school board meeting. The members of the school board are elected by the people in the community. They give final approval on many decisions made by school administrators.

Sometimes, people want to make changes in their local community. For example, a city can decide to cut down trees because they are breaking the sidewalks. If the residents of that neighborhood don't agree with the city, they can present a petition or speak at a City Hall meeting.

People can also help make changes at the state and federal level. People make phone calls, write letters, and send e-mails to their representatives to express their opinions about issues.

Vocabulary

Repeat these words after your teacher. Talk about their meanings. Write the words in your notebook. With a partner, write a sentence using each word.

administrator

approve/approval

influence

issues

opposed

petition

representative

Idiom Watch!
speak out

Remember?
federal state local

☞ **Compare Cultures** With your group, talk about how people make changes in their schools and communities. Compare the US to your home country. Take notes in a chart like this one.

	US	Home Country
School		
Community		

Activity A   Think of something you'd like to change or improve in your school or program. Make a list with your group and vote on the most popular idea.

Activity B   The city wants to let someone build a nightclub in Marlene's neighborhood, and she is not happy about it. With your partner, finish Marlene's conversation with the representative from City Hall. Write the conversation in your notebook.

Marlene: I am opposed to the new nightclub that they want to build in our neighborhood. I think it will cause a lot of problems.

Representative: What kinds of problems are you worried about?

Practice your conversation with your partner.

Activity C   With your partner, choose one of the following situations:

nightclub

fireworks

- You think your child has too much (or too little) homework.
- You want a stop sign at an intersection near your home.
- You want people to stop using fireworks in your city.
- The door at your child's school is left open and unguarded all day.

Decide who you will talk to about the problem, and write a conversation. When you're finished, present your conversation to several pairs of classmates.

Activity D   Interview three classmates. Take notes on their answers to these questions. Report back to your group to share your classmates' answers.

1. Have you ever signed a petition? If so, what kind of petition?
2. If you were opposed to a decision made by your school or city, what would you do?
3. Do you think you can influence change? Give an example.
4. Give an example of something you approve of in your school.
5. Have you ever talked to a school administrator? Explain.
6. Name one federal issue that is important to you right now.

TASK 2: Write a Petition

With your group, write a petition to change something in your school or community. Use Marlene's petition as an example. First explain the problem in one short sentence (see Activity B). Then write a short paragraph that describes the change you want to make. Put numbered lines under the paragraph. Sign your name on the first line. Ask your classmates to sign the petition. Use "would you mind" and "would you consider."

After you finish collecting signatures, have a class discussion about which issues were the most popular and why.

Actions Speak Louder Than Words

◆ Describe positive personal qualities
◆ Use present perfect with *for* and *since*

What qualities do you have that would make you a good employee?

◆ **Reading Tip** When you need to remember important information from a reading, it's a good idea to highlight or underline main ideas. As you read this section of Jenny's resume, underline the skills that would make her a good employee.

arrange

assign

coordinate

direct

donate

COMMUNITY ACTIVITIES

Boyd Park Cleanup I helped organize a project to clean up a neighborhood park. This involved contacting Parks & Recreation for permission, arranging a meeting with neighbors, collecting necessary materials, and assigning responsibilities to various groups.

School Carnival I have helped coordinate the yearly carnival at Melbourne Elementary School for the last three years. This involved asking parents and community members to volunteer and donate materials. I also requested donations of food and prizes from local businesses. I organized a committee to advertise the event.

"No Parking" Petition I helped collect signatures for a petition to require parking permits on Gradwell Street near the hospital. I attended the City Hall meetings where the petition was presented.

Trip Fund-raiser I participated in the candy-sale fund-raiser for the 7th grade Washington, D.C., trip. For this event I collected and kept track of the money brought in from six different classrooms. I helped organize a party for the students and parents who participated in the fund-raiser.

Think of all the projects you have helped with!

Jenny is looking for a job. She hasn't had a job in many years, but she has been involved in several community projects. She knows that this volunteer work will look good on her resume.

Idiom Watch!

Actions speak louder than words.

Talk or Write

1. What kinds of responsibilities do you think Jenny assigned to the Boyd Park volunteers?
2. What kinds of materials do you think parents and community members donated to the school carnival?
3. Which skills would make Jenny a good employee?

Group Chat Use the adjectives in the Vocabulary box to talk about people you have known. Explain why the word describes them.

Have you ever known someone who is persistent?

My friend, Jorge, is very persistent. He has called three times about the job he wants at the mall.

Make a chart like this one. Write the adjectives from the Vocabulary box in the left column. Next to each word, write examples of behavior that show the quality.

Have you ever known someone who is _____?	Examples
persistent	called 3 times about a job

Vocabulary

Repeat these words after your teacher. Talk about their meanings. Write the words in your notebook. With a partner, write a sentence using each word.

arrange

donate

improve

confident

dedicated

generous

outgoing

persistent

punctual

Grammar Talk: Present Perfect with *for* and *since*

He has volunteered at the food bank **for** three months.
She has donated her time to the school **for** many years.
He has participated in the multicultural carnival **for** the last two years.

We have worked to improve the neighborhood **since** June.
I have arranged all of the meetings **since** 2001.
He has been outgoing **since** he was a child.

Find the words for *and* since *in each sentence. Which word is followed by a specific time? Which word is followed by a length of time?*

Pronunciation Target • Stress on Adjectives
🎧 *Listen to your teacher or the audio.*
He has worked here for **ten** months.
I have known him for **many** years.

Notice that the adjective after for *is clearly stressed. Write more sentences with the present perfect and* for, *and practice saying them to your partner.*

Activity A **Group Chat Follow-Up** Look at the chart from your Group Chat. Use the words in the left column to write about people you know.

<u>My friend Jorge is persistent. He has called three times about a job</u>

<u>at the mall.</u>

Activity B In your group, use each of the following time expressions to talk about things that you have done. Everyone should use each expression at least once. Use *for* or *since*.

September	six months	2000	I was a child
many weeks	two years	last summer	a long time

I have come to class on time since September.

I have studied hard for two years.

Activity C Most of us demonstrate certain qualities in one situation but not in another. Choose one of the following qualities: outgoing, generous, dedicated, confident, punctual.

Write five questions to ask your classmates to find out when they have that quality. Record the answers in your notebook.

Most people are not outgoing when they ride the bus, but they are outgoing with their friends.

Outgoing	Yes	No
Do you talk to strangers on the bus?	III	HHT II
Have you ever had a big party at your house?	HHT I	IIII

Share your results with your group. Discuss the results in class.

TASK 3: Make a Personal Qualities Idea Map

Make an idea map like the one below. Use one of the community involvement or household project ideas you discussed in the Group Chat on page 85. Put the idea in the center circle. In the branching circles, write qualities that you demonstrate by becoming involved. Around the qualities, write specific examples of tasks you need to do that show the qualities.

Make a Poster for a Community Project

Prepare a poster about a community project. Follow these steps:

Get Ready

In groups, choose an idea for getting involved or changing something in your community. Write a description of the project. The description should answer the following questions:

- How will the project benefit the community?
- How will it benefit the people who get involved?
- What tasks does the project require?
- How many people will need to help?
- What materials will you need?
- How much will the materials cost?

Do the Work

Write the information on a large poster.

Present

Sometimes city officials organize town hall meetings to discuss important changes in the community. Have a town hall meeting with your class. Select a president to lead the meeting and two secretaries to take notes. Each group will present their project plan. Take a vote on which project the class would like to do first. Have a class discussion about any changes or additions that you want to make to the plan.

Idiom Watch!
team player

Writing Extension Write a letter to a friend. Tell him or her about one of the class projects. Tell why you think it is good.

✎💻 Technology Extra

Use the computer to make a flyer that announces your project and asks for volunteers. Use computer art to make it more interesting. Exchange flyers with another group. Ask questions about anything you do not understand.

Into Your Own Hands

Becoming a Lifelong Learner

Home	Community	Work/School
1	2	3

- ◆ **Vocabulary** Words for learning and planning
- ◆ **Language** Future with *will* and *be going to* • Polite requests with modals
- ◆ **Pronunciation** Reduction of *be* and *will* • Reduction of *would you* and *could you*
- ◆ **Culture** Opportunities for lifelong learning

Why do adults want to continue learning after they finish high school or college?

Anthony Robinson is talking to his 8-year-old son's teacher about problems that his son, Cameron, is having at school. Lately, Cameron's behavior has been poor, and he hasn't been completing his homework. Anthony wants to help his son, but he needs to learn more about his son's behavior.

Think and Talk

1. What do you see in the photograph?
2. What do you think that Anthony is saying to the teacher?
3. What can Anthony do to learn more about his son's problem?
4. If you want to learn more about a topic, where can you get information or who can you talk to?

What's Your Opinion? Many people go to doctors and teachers for advice. Do you think doctors and teachers always give good advice? Explain your answer.

Dictation 🎧 Listen to your teacher or the audio. Write the sentences that you hear.

Gather Your Thoughts There are many reasons for being a lifelong learner. Some reasons are practical and others are personal. What is practical for one person might not be practical for another person.

Use the idea map below to brainstorm topics that you could learn more about. Decide why you want to learn more about the topics. Write where you can learn more about them.

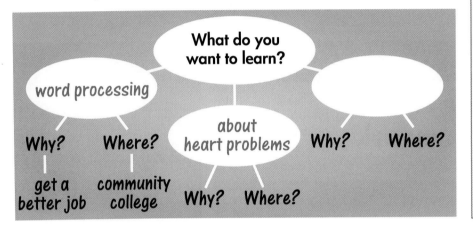

Vocabulary

Repeat these words after your teacher. Talk about their meanings. Write the words in your notebook. With a partner, write a sentence using each word.

advantage

career

lifelong learning

opportunity

fulfilling

meaningful

practical

resource

enroll/enrollment

register/registration

Idiom Watch!

take something into your own hands

What's the Problem? Look at your idea map again. What things can get in the way of becoming a lifelong learner? Think or talk with a partner.

Setting Goals Think about things you want to be able to do to continue learning. Which goals are most important to you? Rank them from 1 (most important) to 6.

_____ **a.** talk about future plans

_____ **b.** learn ways to improve study habits

_____ **c.** learn how to use library resources

_____ **d.** learn how to ask politely for information or help

_____ **e.** understand recorded enrollment procedures for college

_____ **f.** another goal: _____

Which was the most important goal for your class? Tally your answers. Talk about your most important goals.

Study Habits

◆ Learn ways to improve study habits
◆ Use future tense with *will* and *be going to*

What were your study habits like when you were a child? Have they changed?

consistent
daydream
distraction
encourage

◆ **Reading Tip** Thinking about the title of an article can help prepare you for reading. Look at the title of the reading. What do you think this article is about? Read the article for one minute. When the minute is over, close your book. With your partner, write down as many ideas as you can remember.

PARENTS' CORNER

The Dog Ate My Homework

Do you get notes from your child's teachers complaining about incomplete work or daydreaming? Does your child always make excuses for not doing homework?

There are many things you can do to help your child study. You need to get organized, be consistent, and avoid distractions. The biggest distraction from homework is the TV. Turn it off. Friends and family members can also be a distraction.

Be sure that your child has a quiet study area. Organize the study area. Make sure that all necessary supplies are nearby. The desk or table should be large enough to hold all of the materials. Good lighting is important.

It's a good idea to put up a bulletin board to keep track of school projects and events. Keep a book for writing down assignments. Teach your child how to organize a notebook by subjects and dates.

Being consistent is important for good study habits. Study in the same place and at the same time every day. Be positive about studying and encourage your child.

If you are a student yourself, or are thinking about going back to school, you might find that these studying tips are good for learners of all ages.

Talk or Write
1. Now read the article more carefully. Which ideas did you forget?
2. Would any of these suggestions help you with your studying? Which ones?

Idiom Watch!
make excuses

Group Chat Think about your plans for your education. Ask your group members the questions in the chart.

What's your name?	What are you going to do in the future?
Taylor	take computer classes

Grammar Talk: Future with *will* and *be going to*

I'm going to study at the library tomorrow.

I think **I'll study** at the library tomorrow.

I'll help you study.

I'll come home early.

We use will *and* be going to *for planned activities. We use* will *to make offers and promises.*

You can write contractions of will *and* be *with pronouns, but not with nouns.*

Pronunciation Target • Reduction of *be* and *will*

🎧 *Listen to your teacher or the audio. Notice that the helping verbs* be *and* will *are normally reduced in spoken English. Going to* is often reduced to *gonna in speech, but it cannot be spelled that way. Practice the sentences with your partner.*

I'm not going to make excuses.
She's not going to fall behind in her studies.
They're going to make studying a priority.
He thinks he'll change his schedule.
She'll try to be consistent.

Vocabulary

Repeat these words after your teacher. Talk about their meanings. Write the words in your notebook. With a partner, write a sentence using each word.

consistent/inconsistent
distract/distraction

priority
routine
schedule

Idiom Watch!
catch up
fall behind

Activity A 🎧 Listen to your teacher or the audio. Write the sentences that you hear. Your teacher will reduce *will* and *going to*. Don't write the reduced forms.

Activity B Read the conversation. Underline the future verbs.

Grant: What are you going to do tomorrow?
Garrett: I'm going to move my desk into the other room.
Grant: That's a good idea. I'll help you.

With your partner, write a conversation. Use *be going to* to tell about a plan and *will* to make an offer or a promise.

Activity C **Group Chat Follow-Up** Look at the chart from your Group Chat. Write sentences about your group members in your notebook.

Taylor is going to take computer classes.

Activity D Interview three classmates about their study habits. Take notes on their answers. Report back to your group to compare answers.
1. Are you consistent or inconsistent about studying English? Why?
2. Do you have a study routine? What is it?
3. Do you ever fall behind in your work? How do you catch up?
4. Describe your daily schedule.
5. Are there any distractions in your study area? What are they?
6. Do you ever make excuses for not studying? Give an example.
7. Is studying a priority for you? Explain your answer.

 TASK 1: Make a Study Plan

Write a plan for improving your own study habits. List changes that you could make in your routine or study area that would help you with your English or with another subject that you study. Write each change in the correct place in a chart like this one.

Changes in Routine	Changes in Study Area
get up earlier	clean my desk

Get Informed

- ◆ Use library resources
- ◆ Ask polite questions

Have you ever looked for information at a library? How did you find the materials?

◆ **Reading Tip** When you research a topic, it is often important to find the most recent information. Look at the date of each publication in the list below.

index

issue

periodical

publisher

vol.

Book Index

1. *Attention Deficit Hyperactivity Disorder* Ackerman, Paula; New York: Village Books c1999 223p

2. *Helping Your ADHD Child* Jenson, Samuel; New Jersey: Market Press c2003 152p

Periodical Index

1. "Does Your Child Really Need Medication?" By: George, Erby; *Family Health* 12/13/02, Vol. 31 Issue 110, p.25, 2p.

2. "Study Tips for ADHD Children" By: Wong, Eric; *Arizona Educator* 2/18/91, Vol. 23 Issue 96, p.34, 1p.

The pediatrician told Anthony that Cameron might have Attention Deficit Hyperactivity Disorder (ADHD), which makes it difficult for children to concentrate. Anthony is going to research ADHD on his own.

Talk or Write

1. Which article is more than 10 years old?
2. Who is the publisher of the second book? Where was it published?
3. What is the name of the first periodical?
4. What is the title of the article in *Family Health?*
5. What page does "Study Tips for ADHD Children" begin on? How long is it?
6. Which articles or books would be most useful for Anthony?

Group Chat Libraries are a valuable resource for researching topics of interest. What do you know about your local library? Discuss the following questions with your group and take notes on a chart like this one.

Could you please tell me where the library is?	
Do you know when the library is open?	
Could you tell me how to get a library card?	

Share your answers with the class and make a class chart on the board.

Vocabulary

Repeat these words after your teacher. Talk about their meanings. Write the words in your notebook. With a partner, write a sentence using each word.

article
biography
documentary
nonfiction
periodical

due
overdue
reference
renew
research

Grammar Talk: Polite Requests with Modals

These questions are direct:
Where is the reference section?
What does this word mean?

These questions are more polite:
Could you please tell me **where** the reference section is?
Would you please tell me **what** this word means?

Compare the direct question to the polite question. What happens to the verb?

Pronunciation Target • Reduction of *would you* and *could you*
🎧 *Listen to your teacher or the audio. You will hear the sentences from the grammar box. Notice how the sound changes when* would you *and* could you *are said at normal speed.*

Idiom Watch!
look up
check out

Activity A Ask your classmates for help. Use "Would you/Could you please tell me" or "Would you/Could you please show me" in your questions.

Could you please show me where the pencil sharpener is?

Would you please tell me when the class ends?

Activity B **Group Chat Follow-Up** Look at the chart from your Group Chat. In your notebook, write what you learned.

<u>There is a small library near the school. It is open on Sunday.</u>

Activity C Fill in the blanks with words from the Vocabulary box on page 100. Compare your answers with your group.

1. I need to talk to the librarian. Could you tell me where the _____ desk is?

2. Could you tell me when these books are _____ ?

3. Can I _____ these books over the phone?

4. I'd like to watch this _____. Would you please show me how the VCR works?

5. Do you know if this magazine has an _____ on ADHD?

6. These books are _____ . Could you tell me how much I owe?

7. I'm looking for a magazine. Could you show me the _____ index?

8. I'd like to do some _____ on a medical problem. Could you please help me get started?

TASK 2: Narrow Down a Topic

Talk to your group. Brainstorm three or more specific examples for each topic:

Biographies   Self-Help   Health   Politics
Personal Finance   History   Travel   Sports

Idiom Watch!
narrow down

Elvis Presley was a singer.

Choose three topics. In your notebook, make a chart like this. Under each topic, write three specific things within that topic that interest you. Tell your partner something you know about each example.

Topic: Biographies	Topic: Self-Help	Topic:
1. Elvis Presley	1. Losing weight	1.
2. Benjamin Franklin	2. Getting organized	2.
3. Nelson Mandela	3. Dealing with sorrow	3.

Back to School

- ◆ Understand enrollment procedures
- ◆ Learn about adult education in the US

Describe the enrollment process at schools you know.

◆ **Listening Tip** 🎧 Listening for specific information can help you understand what you hear. The recording will explain how to do the tasks below. The tasks are not in order. You can read the words on page 120.

development
drop
followed by
psychology

Anthony became interested in ADHD. He's going to enroll in a class on child development. He is going to enroll over the phone. He is listening to the instructions for phone registration.

Talk or Write As you listen again, sequence the tasks from 1 to 6.

pound key = #
star key = *

_____ add another class

_____ enter personal ID number

__1__ enter student ID number

_____ add a class

_____ drop a class

_____ review schedule

In the US   Lifelong Learning

The United States offers many opportunities for lifelong learning. Many school districts have adult schools where adults can earn high-school diplomas or study computers and other work-related subjects. There are also many private schools where students can learn a particular skill, such as secretarial skills or electronics. There are community or city colleges in most areas. Students can get two-year degrees in many subjects or can take classes that prepare them for a college or university that offers four-year degrees and graduate degrees. These colleges and universities have higher tuition and more requirements for admission than other schools.

It is never too late for adults in the US to go back to school. Sometimes people are interested in learning about a specific subject. Sometimes people want more training so that they can earn more money on their job. Many people change careers and return to school to get a new degree. People who didn't go to college often decide later in life that they want to get a college degree. Sometimes retired people go back to school because they have always wanted to, but they've never had enough time or money before.

Vocabulary

Repeat these words after your teacher. Talk about their meanings. Write the words in your notebook. With a partner, write a sentence using each word.

admission

fee

requirement

tuition

add

drop

earn

☛ **Compare Cultures** Fill in a chart like this one with information about your home country. Then talk to your group about the educational system in your country.

Home Country _____	
Do people often change careers?	
Do people often go back to school?	
Are there adult schools?	
Are universities expensive?	

Activity A   Are you planning to study something besides English? Tell your group.

I'm going to study computers at the adult school.

I want to be a teacher someday.

Activity B Look at the following answers to questions someone might ask at a college admissions office. With your partner, practice asking the questions and giving the answers. Use the polite form for questions. If possible, use a word from the Vocabulary box on page 103 in each question.

Could you please tell me how I can drop a class?

During the first month, just tell the teacher you don't want to attend anymore.

1. During the first month, just tell the teacher you don't want to attend anymore.
2. It's $350 a semester.
3. You can learn computer repair and many other skills at the adult school.
4. You need to pay $25 with your application. You'll also need to pay for your books.
5. You can get your diploma by taking all of the units you need. It will take two years if you attend full-time.
6. You won't get a refund.
7. You need to have a high school diploma, and you need to live in the area.
8. Just turn in your application by May 10.

TASK 3: Write about a Topic of Interest

Look at the list of classes. Talk with your class about what the abbreviations mean. Choose which class is most interesting to you and explain why to your group. Tell which one you would least like to take and why.

Course No.	Course Name	Course No.	Course Name
PSY 321	Intro to Child Development	NURS 31	Intro to Nursing
BUS 101	Intro to Business	DENT 22	Intro to Dental Technology
ACCT 211	Intro to Accounting	MEDT 30	Intro to Medical Office
HOME 224	Intro to Fashion Design	AUTO 15	Intro to Auto Technology
INDUS 200	Intro to Carpentry	NUTR 12	Intro to Nutrition
COMP 102	Intro to Computers	HORT 50	Intro to Landscaping

Write a paragraph. In your topic sentence, tell which course is most interesting to you. Then explain why you think it's interesting. Think about these questions to help you get started. Are you interested in the subject for practical reasons? If so, how would learning about this subject be useful to you? Are you interested in the subject for personal reasons? If so, why would learning about this subject be meaningful to you?

Intro = the first course in the subject (introduction)

Make a Research Action Plan

Make a plan to research an important topic. Follow these steps:

Get Ready

Choose a topic that is important to you and that you would like to learn more about, for example, a health problem, something you want to make, or a place you want to visit.

Do the Work

Complete the outline at the right to make a plan of action for learning more about your topic.

Present

Share your outline with a partner from your group. If your partner has more ideas, add them to the outline. When you and your partner are finished, meet with a pair from a different group to present your outlines.

Writing Extension Use your outline to write your plan of action. Explain your learning project, who you will talk to, where you will go for information, and what search terms you will use. Include any changes you need to make in your routine or learning environment in order to help you with this project.

1. People you can talk to who know about the subject (the doctor, a teacher, the clerk at the hardware store, a classmate who has been to the place that I want to visit . . .).

2. Search words you can use at the library and on the Internet to get information on this subject (ADD, Attention Deficit Disorder, ADD medicine). If you put in search words that are too general, you might get too much information. Include specific search words in your list to narrow down the topic.

3. Places you can go to learn more about the subject, with names and phone numbers (local community colleges, City Hall, University extension, library, Parks & Recreation department, etc.)

4. Changes you might need to make in your habits, schedule, or environment for your plan to be successful.

Technology Extra

Search the Internet for books about your topic. There are many bookstores online.
You can search for subjects and titles that interest you at the bookstore web sites.

Keeping Up with the Times

Dealing with Change

Work/School 1   Community 2   Home 3

◆ **Vocabulary** Words about dealing with change

◆ **Language** Present perfect continuous • Present/future sentences with *if*

◆ **Pronunciation** Primary and secondary stress • List intonation

◆ **Culture** Changing workplaces

When was the last time you had to learn something new? How did you feel?

Rania has worked at the sewing factory for 10 years. Her company is going to make some changes. She is concerned about the changes at her workplace.

Think and Talk

1. What do you see in the photograph?
2. What changes at work do you think Rania is concerned about?
3. Why do you think she is concerned?
4. Are there changes happening in your life that you are concerned about or happy about? Explain your answer.

What's Your Opinion? Many people are afraid of or nervous about changes that happen in their lives. They'll do anything to avoid change. Give an example of when it's OK to avoid change and when it's important to accept change.

Dictation 🎧 Listen to your teacher or the audio. You will hear sentences about changes. Write the sentences. When you finish, correct them with the class. Talk about the sentences with your partner. Do you agree with them? Are they true for you?

Gather Your Thoughts In your group, brainstorm examples of changes that happen in people's lives. Categorize them in a chart like the one below. Decide which kind of change in each category would be the most difficult to deal with. Put a check by that example.

Personal/Home	School	Workplace	Community
get engaged	graduate	new boss	bank closes

Make a class list of changes from each group's chart. Copy the list in your notebook. You will use the ideas from *School* and *Workplace* for your Lesson 1 Group Chat.

What's the Problem? Look at the examples of life changes in the class chart. Why are these changes sometimes difficult? How can people deal with each change? Think or talk with a partner.

Setting Goals Think about how you deal with change in your life. Which goals are most important to you? Rank them from 1 (most important) to 6.

_____ **a.** discuss pros and cons

_____ **b.** explain how to use something

_____ **c.** describe the effects of technology

_____ **d.** discuss my feelings about different kinds of changes

_____ **e.** give a presentation

_____ **f.** another goal: _____

Which was the most important goal for your class? Tally your answers. Talk about your most important goals.

Vocabulary

Repeat these words after your teacher. Talk about their meanings. Write the words in your notebook. With a partner, write a sentence using each word.

pros and cons

adapt
confront
cope
overcome
react/reaction
resist

Idiom Watch!
keep up with the times
look forward to
deal with

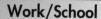
Go with the Flow

◆ Describe pros and cons
◆ Use present perfect continuous

demands
outdated
outweigh
production
technician
workshop

When you are going to make a change, do you think carefully about the pros and cons, or do you make quick decisions?

◆ **Reading Tip** Having a purpose for reading helps you focus on important ideas. This memo discusses the pros and cons of buying new sewing machines. As you read, count how many pros and cons there are in the memo.

Memo from the Manager

We have been using outdated machines for several years now. Since March, management has been weighing the pros and cons of purchasing computerized sewing machines for all sewing technicians.

Our outdated machines have hurt production and sales. Although the machines work fine, they are not efficient. They cannot keep up with production demands. In addition, it is not possible to make creative designs. The computerized machines would allow us to create new designs and compete with larger companies. Even though we don't have enough money to pay for the new machines, we have enough to cover 75%. The profit from increased production would pay for the machines.

Because the pros outweigh the cons, we have decided to purchase the new machines. We expect the computerized machines to arrive next month. A workshop for all sewing technicians will be scheduled when the new equipment arrives. All sewing technicians are required to attend.

Idiom Watch!

go with the flow

weigh pros and cons

Rania has been doing the same type of work for many years. She received this memo from Human Resources.

Talk or Write

1. What is the purpose of this memo?
2. Why did the company decide to buy new sewing machines?
3. List the pros and cons of the new purchase.
4. How could the company afford to pay for the new machines?
5. Should the company ask employees to learn the new machines?

Group Chat Changes at work and school—like getting a new teacher, changing your work schedule, or moving to a new job location—have many different effects on your life. With your group, use the chart below to talk about the effects of these changes. Write the changes on the left. Write the effects of the changes on the right.

What changes have been happening at your work or school?	What effects have the changes had on you?
new class	meet new people

Vocabulary

Repeat these words after your teacher. Talk about their meanings. Write the words in your notebook. With a partner, write a sentence using each word.

affect

train

update

effect

reaction

workshop

mandatory

outdated

Grammar Talk: Present Perfect Continuous

Rania **has been sewing** for many years.

The employees **have been using** outdated machines for a long time.

The company **hasn't been updating** their equipment.

Rania **has been feeling** nervous about the new machines at work.

The present perfect continuous is used to describe actions that began in the past and are still happening now or have just stopped. A present perfect continuous verb has three parts. Underline them in the sentences.

Pronunciation Target • Primary and Secondary Stress

🎧 *Listen to your teacher or the audio. Repeat the sentences.*

I've **real**ly been working hard.
These ma**chines** are really outdated.
They've been **plan**ning the workshop for months.
The **work**shop is mandatory for Rania.

In a sentence with several stressed syllables, the first stressed syllable is usually the strongest. Repeat the sentences several times.

Activity A   Tell your partner what you have been doing lately. Use the present perfect continuous. Then, listen to your partner. Tell your group what your partner has been doing lately.

Write one sentence about each person in your group. Underline the primary stress in the sentences. Circle the three parts of the verb.

> What have you been doing lately?
>
> I've been looking for a job.
>
> Kyung Suk has been training in the computer lab.

Activity B   Listen to your teacher or the audio. Write the sentences in your notebook. Read each sentence out loud with your partner. Write *T (true)* or *F (false)* after each sentence. Correct the false sentences.

Activity C   As a group, discuss the pros and cons of these situations. Make a list of pros and cons for each situation. Do the pros outweigh the cons?

1. becoming the boss
2. starting a new job
3. going back to school
4. working long hours

Activity D   **Group Chat Follow-Up**   Look at the chart from your Group Chat on page 109. In your notebook, write about the pros and cons of one change.

I have a class. I've met a lot of new friends. I haven't been seeing my old friends.

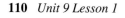 **TASK 1:**   Weigh the Pros and Cons

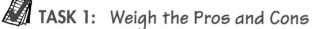

Workplaces occasionally update technology. They buy new phone systems, computers, and machines. With your class, choose a workplace. Write pros and cons of new technology there. Debate the issue with a partner.

> debate
>
> scanner

One Step Up
Volunteer to debate the issue in front of the class.

Pros	Cons
1. Bar code scanners speed up the work for cashiers.	1. When the scanner doesn't work, employees don't know the prices.
2.	2.
3.	3.

Learn New Technology

◆ Learn about changing technology in the US
◆ Describe useful technology

Think of a machine or a piece of equipment that you know how to use. How did you learn to use it?

| clerical |
| manufacture |
| retail |

◆ **Reading Tip** Scanning is a useful tool for finding specific information quickly. Look at the graph quickly to see which business has used the most new technology in the last five years.

Percentage of Businesses in Roseville County Using New Technology in the Last Five Years

Business	Percentage
Manufacturing	40%
Medical Facilities	65%
Education	30%
Government Offices	28%
Retail Stores	32%
Clerical/Administrative Offices	40%
Restaurants	20%

0% 10% 20% 30% 40% 50% 60% 70%

Many businesses are purchasing new technology. Soon Rania will use a computerized sewing machine at work. Now her bank has a new type of ATM.

Talk or Write

1. Ask your partner questions about the graph.
2. With your class, brainstorm a list of businesses or jobs that fit into each category.

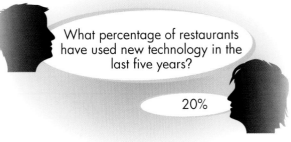

What percentage of restaurants have used new technology in the last five years?

20%

In the US   A Flexible Economy

Being flexible means being willing to accept change. Economic change is very common in the US, so people often say that the US has a flexible economy. One change that affects the economy is that people move a lot. In the US, most people move several times in their lives. People often move because they want to change jobs. They are willing to move where the work is. Even when people don't move to a new place, they often change jobs.

In a flexible economy, people can start new businesses easily. If you have money, you can start a small business in the US with very little red tape. A lot of small businesses fail, but people in the US are not ashamed of having a business that fails. Many people start several businesses before they are successful.

One result of all this flexibility is that employers expect employees to keep up with changes in technology. Most workers are not protected by *seniority,* the number of years on the job, and they must be willing to learn and change with the company if they want to keep their jobs. Even nontechnical employees have been learning how to use new technology. In many cases, it makes their jobs much easier. For example, more and more companies are using bar code scanning technology for shopping and identification. Office computers are connected to networks that make it easier for people to communicate with each other. Waiters and waitresses use touch-screen displays for turning in their orders to the kitchen. Because new technology is appearing in almost every workplace, it has become more and more important to keep up with the times.

Repeat these words after your teacher. Talk about their meanings. Write the words in your notebook. With a partner, write a sentence using each word.

> bar code
>
> display
>
> network
>
> scanning
>
> touch screen

Idiom Watch!
red tape
lay off

☛ **Compare Cultures** Compare the economy of your home country with the economy of the US by discussing these questions with your group.

• How often do people move?

• Is it common to move far away from the family?

• Is it easy for employers to lay off or fire employees?

• Is it easy or difficult to start a new business?

• Is there a lot of new technology?

One Step Up
In groups, discuss the pros and cons of the flexibility in the US economy. Write as many pros and cons as you can.

Activity A Talk to your group about kinds of technology that you or someone you know can use. Share your ideas with the class and make a list on poster paper. Display the list in your classroom. Walk around and ask your classmates what they can use and how long they've been using it. Ask about the items on the class poster.

Can you use a sewing machine?

Yes, I can.

How long have you been using one?

Five years.

Activity B With your group, talk about how technology has affected places in your community. Brainstorm technology changes that have happened in the past 20 years and technology changes that have been happening lately.

With your class, write your ideas in a two-column chart on the board. Use present perfect and present perfect continuous sentences. Put them under these headings:

In the past 20 years, gas stations have added automatic payment machines.

Stores have been putting more products on the Internet lately.

In the Past 20 Years	Lately

TASK 2: Rank the Effects of Technology in the Community

With your group, make a list of technologies that have had an effect on your community. Rank the items on the list in order of importance. Number 1 is the most important.

Explain to the class the reasons for your number 1 choice.

Do a class tally of the number 1 choices.

One Step Up
Make a chart of jobs or businesses that have disappeared due to technology and jobs or businesses that have been unaffected by technology.

We think the scanners at the supermarket are the most important because everyone goes shopping a lot, and it's much faster with the scanners.

Three Cheers!

- ◆ Describe the benefits of technology
- ◆ Use present/future sentences with *if*

What have you learned that has made you feel successful?

◆ **Listening Tip** 🎧 Listening for *key* words can help you focus your attention on the main idea. Listen to your teacher or the audio. As you listen, write down words that describe Rania's success. You can read the words on page 120.

admire

promote

system

Idiom Watch!

make a toast

open new doors

put your mind to something

Three cheers!

Rania's friends are celebrating her success. Jason is making a toast.

Talk or Write

1. How has Rania been successful?
2. What are her future plans?
3. Why does Jason admire Rania?
4. What doors were opened for Rania?
5. What kind of person is Rania? Think of three adjectives to describe her.

What's Your Opinion? Some people are jealous when other people succeed. Can you explain why? How can people avoid being jealous?

Group Chat If you learn something new, it will keep your brain active and make you feel good. Talk to your group about things that you have already learned how to do. Ask your group these questions. Write information about the group in a chart.

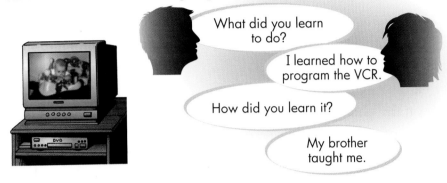

What did you learn to do?

I learned how to program the VCR.

How did you learn it?

My brother taught me.

What did you learn to do?	How did you learn it?	If I want to learn it, can you teach me?
program VCR	brother	yes

Grammar Talk: Present/Future Sentences with *if*

If I **put** this in the microwave, it **will explode.**

If he **doesn't check** the answering machine, he **won't know** when I'm coming home.

I'll be late if I **don't figure out** how to set the alarm clock.

I **won't bother** you anymore if you **teach** me how to use this program.

Which verb is in the part of the sentence with if, *the present verb or the future verb? When do sentences with* if *need a comma?*

Activity A **Group Chat Follow-Up** Look at your Group Chat chart. Use the information to write sentences with *if* in your notebook.

If I want to learn how to program the VCR, Don can teach me.

Vocabulary

Repeat these words after your teacher. Talk about their meanings. Write the words in your notebook. With a partner, write a sentence using each word.

clockwise/
counterclockwise

adjust

hang up

operate

press

program

remove

set

start over

turn

Idiom Watch!
figure out

One Step Up
With your partner, talk about things that have made you feel successful. These could be things you have learned how to do, goals you have reached, jobs you have done, or things you do well every day. Write a toast to your partner. Start like this: *"Here's to (name) _____."* Stand up with your group to toast your partner. Don't forget to raise your glass!

Activity B Continue your partner's sentences as shown to the right: Start with number 1. Continue until everyone in the group has spoken. Then start over with number 2.

1. If I study hard,
2. If I set my watch,
3. If you program your VCR,
4. If you hang up on your friend,
5. If you remove the batteries in a flashlight,
6. If you press the wrong button on the phone,

If I study hard, I'll learn a lot of English.

If I learn a lot of English, I'll get a better job.

If I get a better job, I'll make more money.

If I make more money, I'll buy a new car.

Pronunciation Target • Intonation in Lists

🎧 *Listen to your teacher or the audio.*

I have a computer(▲), a cell phone(▲), a microwave(▲), and a radio(▼).

Where does the intonation rise? Where does it fall?

Make a sentence that lists four things that you have. Mark the intonation. Say your sentence to four different classmates.

Activity C Make a chart with five columns in your notebook. Write these five questions at the top of the columns.

1. What things in your house do you set?
2. What things do you adjust?
3. What things in your house have buttons?
4. What things in your house have dials?
5. What things in your house have batteries?

Walk around the class. Ask your classmates these questions. Each time someone gives you a new answer, write it under the question.

TASK 3: Find Someone Who Can Help You

List five things that you want to learn about using technology. Make a chart like this one. Write what you want to learn in the left column. Ask classmates if they know how to do those things. Then write the names of the people who can help you.

What I Want to Learn	Who Can Help Me
make bread in a breadmaker	Ana

Teach How to Use Something

Teach your group how to use an item of technology. Follow these steps:

Get Ready

1. Choose one form of technology from home, work, or community. This should be something that you like.
2. Look at the instructions one student wrote for using his clock radio.

Do the Work

1. Answer the following questions:
   - How long does it take to learn how to use this technology?
   - How often do you use it?
   - What are the costs?
   - Has it made your life easier?
2. Write out the steps for using the item.
3. Bring in the item or draw a picture of it.
4. Practice your presentation with your partner.

---

1. To set the time, just press the hour button and the minute button until you get to the right time.

2. To set the alarm, hold down the alarm set button and press the hour button until you get to the right hour. Repeat with the minute button. If you are setting the alarm for the morning, be sure to check that the AM light is showing!

3. To turn up the sound, turn the volume dial clockwise.

4. If you want to sleep a little more after the alarm rings, press the snooze button.

5. Replace the batteries every year. If the power goes out or if you unplug the clock, the batteries will keep the right time on the clock.

6. Turn the tuning dial to get the radio station that you like.

Present

First, introduce your topic. You can use the answers to the questions above as your introduction. Then teach your group how to use the item by showing them the parts and explaining the steps.

Be sure to congratulate your partners when they have successfully completed their presentations.

Writing Extension Choose one of these areas of technology: medical, household, or transportation. Write about what changes we might see in that area. Use your imagination. Do the possible changes frighten you? Are you excited about them?

✎💻 Technology Extra

Find a picture of your item of technology on the Internet. Copy it into a document.
Type the steps for using the item.

Listening Scripts

This section contains scripts for passages on which listening lessons are based and for listening activities based on dialogues. It does not include other listening activities or Pronunciation Targets. Complete scripts for the content of the *English—No Problem!* audiotape and audio CD for level 3 are found in the *Teacher's Edition*.

UNIT 1
Closing the Gap

Lesson 1, page 12

Recording: Thank you for calling the Springfield Community Center. If you would like information about our location and hours, press *1*. If you are interested in a schedule of youth activities, press *2*. For adult special-interest classes, press *3*. For a schedule of activities for seniors, press *4*. If you would like to speak to an operator, press *0*, or stay on the line. To hear these options again, press *5*.

The Community Center offers activities for seniors, fifty and older, Monday through Saturday. Activities include exercise and craft classes, sports and games, travel opportunities, special-interest clubs, movies, and health lectures. To receive a brochure with a complete schedule of activities, please leave your name and address after the tone.

Mina: Could you please send me a brochure? My name is Mina Patel, that's P-A-T-E-L. My address is 2430 Ely Avenue, that's E-L-Y. Springfield, Washington 98321. Thank you very much.

UNIT 2
Smoothing Things Over

Lesson 3, page 30

Jae Lee: How's it going, Sarah?
Sarah: Oh, I'm fine, except that I just made a fool of myself in Tae Kwon Do class.
Koji: What did you do?
Sarah: Well, I was just goofing around with my friend in back of class, you know, talking and laughing. We used to be in the same aerobics class, and we had a lot of fun. But Tae Kwon Do is a martial art. Our teacher wants us to take it seriously.
Jae Lee: What did he do?
Sarah: He talked about appropriate behavior in a martial arts class and I was so embarrassed! I'm an adult! I should know better.
Koji: You've never taken Tae Kwon Do before, Sarah, so you didn't know what they expected. Give yourself a break!
Jae Lee: Believe me, I know what it's like to make a mistake, too. I think that I offended my neighbor yesterday.
Koji: Oh yeah. Did you talk to her about that?
Jae Lee: Yes, I did. That was good advice. I went over to her house later that day and told her that I hoped I didn't offend her. I explained that it surprised me when she hugged me. She wasn't offended, and she was glad that I came over to talk about it. Maybe you should talk to your teacher, Sarah. It made me feel better!
Sarah: I think I will. And I'm going to apologize!

UNIT 3
Better Safe Than Sorry

Lesson 3, page 42
Officer Murphy: Can you tell me what happened?

Miguel: Well, two guys asked what time it was, and I said, "Sorry, I don't wear a watch." Then, they asked the same question to an older couple sitting next to me. All of a sudden, the woman was screaming to the man, "Don't give him your wallet! Don't give them anything!" Then, one guy grabbed the woman's purse and they both ran away.
Officer Murphy: Can you describe the suspects? What did they look like?
Miguel: They were young. They looked like teenagers. One was about my height. The other one was taller. I didn't really notice their faces.
Officer Murphy: What were they wearing?
Miguel: They were both wearing jeans. The taller one had a black t-shirt on, and I think the other one was wearing a green jacket.
Officer Murphy: The victims didn't get a good look at them. Were there any other witnesses?
Miguel: Some people were around, but they went inside after it happened.
Officer Murphy: Did anyone try to help?
Miguel: I tried to run after the two guys, but they got away. Then I came back to see if the people were OK.
Officer Murphy: Thank you for your information. You've been a lot of help.

Activity C, page 44
Listen to the 911 emergency call.
Operator: 911. What is your emergency?
Man: My neighbor fell down our stairs, and he can't move.
Operator: Is he breathing?
Man: Yes, he's crying in pain.
Operator: Is he bleeding?

Man: No, I don't see any blood.
Operator: OK, don't move him. Stay with him. Tell me your address and give me the major cross streets near your home.
Man: 445 West Palmdale Avenue near Glendale Boulevard and Bell Avenue.
Operator: Stay calm. The ambulance will be right there.

UNIT 4
Planning Ahead

Lesson 2, page 51
Agent: Thank you for meeting with me, Mr. and Mrs. Morales. I have a lot of information for you about insuring your home.
Victor: Oh, we don't have to get insurance. We don't own this house. We're renting.
Olivia: But I asked him to come talk to us about renters insurance, Victor. One of the women at work recommended him.
Victor: I've never heard of renters insurance. Doesn't the landlord have to cover everything?
Agent: Actually, no. Imagine you come home one day to find that someone broke into your apartment and damaged your belongings. Or what if you walked into your living room and found your furniture in several inches of water? Your landlord wouldn't pay for that.
Victor: But our things aren't worth very much.
Agent: Maybe, but would you be able to replace your valuables if they were stolen?
Olivia: No, we wouldn't. Which things are covered?
Agent: Your stereo, furniture, television, jewelry, computer, bicycles, and other belongings are all covered.

Victor: We haven't really had any problems with theft around here.
Agent: That's good. Your premiums are lower if you live in a safe neighborhood. But renters insurance doesn't only cover stolen items. It also covers damage from fire or smoke, lightning, explosions, windstorms, and water damage from plumbing.
Olivia: This is very interesting.
Victor: Yeah, well, we need to talk it over. We'll get back to you.

Activity C, page 53
Olivia: How much does renters insurance cost?
Agent: You've got to think about how much your belongings are worth. For example, if you want $30,000 worth of coverage, you have to spend about $200 a year. For replacement insurance, you must pay a little more.
Olivia: What's replacement insurance?
Agent: The company will pay you enough money to buy new belongings. Without replacement insurance, the company only has to pay what your belongings are worth now. For example, your five-year-old TV may only be worth $50, but if you have to buy a new one, you'll spend a lot more.

UNIT 5
Making Ends Meet

Lesson 2, page 63
Why pay department store prices when you can have the same brand-name clothing at half the cost or less? At Second-Hand Rose, you'll find nearly new clothing to satisfy all of your fashion needs. We take pride in choosing only the latest styles and top labels. Each item is

carefully inspected for quality and appeal. Treat yourself to the coolest clothes, the hottest shoes, and the wildest accessories. You'll find us at the corner of Rose and Magnolia. We're open Wednesday through Sunday, nine to nine. Second-Hand Rose. Just for you, better than new!

Activity C, page 65
Salesperson: May I help you?
Gail: Yes. I'd like to return these sunglasses.
Salesperson: What's the problem?
Gail: They're scratched!
Salesperson: Oh, I see. Would you like a refund or an exchange?
Gail: I'd like to exchange them.
Salesperson: No problem. I'll get you some new ones.

UNIT 6
Facing Problems Head On

Lesson 3, page 78
I'd like you to take a moment to think about these questions:
- Is drinking or drug use making your home life unhappy?
- Have you had financial problems as a result of drinking or drug use?
- Do you crave a drink or drugs at a certain time of the day?
- Has drinking or using drugs caused problems at your job or business?
- Do you drink or use drugs to escape from worries or troubles?
- Do you drink or use drugs alone?
- Have you ever had complete loss of memory from drinking or using drugs?

If you have answered YES to any of the above questions, you may need help. And the New Life Substance Abuse Center is here to help you.

We offer both residential and outpatient services to men and women who wish to recover from substance abuse and rebuild their lives. We respect your dignity and your privacy. Most insurance plans will cover the cost of treatment services. Your new life can begin today. Call now.

UNIT 7
Pitching In

Lesson 1, page 84

Marlene: I can't believe what has happened to the park. It used to be so clean. But now I don't even like to walk there because there's so much trash everywhere. The graffiti in the bathrooms and on the buildings is horrible. It's an eyesore! I want to do something about it.

Jenny: OK, Mom. I know what you're thinking. You already have a plan, don't you?

Marlene: Well, I've made a list of all the different jobs that need to be done to clean the park up.

Jenny: Isn't that the city's responsibility?

Marlene: Maybe it is. But I don't want to wait. I want to help clear the litter, get rid of the graffiti, and clean things up.

Jenny: How can we clean the whole park, Mom? It's so big!

Marlene: We need to get the neighbors involved. Maybe if they help us clean the park up, they'll be more interested in keeping it clean. Would you help me get this started?

Jenny: Well, I'm not really sure that we should do this, Mom. Don't we need permission?

Marlene: Yes. You could call Parks & Recreation. Or you could start talking to neighbors.

Jenny: I'll take Parks & Recre-ation. You visit the neighbors.

Marlene: OK. And maybe you could ask the kids to give us a hand.

Jenny: I can't even get them to clean their rooms!

UNIT 8
Into Your Own Hands

Lesson 3, page 102

Welcome to the Fredonia Community College Telephone Registration System. Before you register, you will need a copy of your class schedule, your student ID number, and your Personal Identification Number. If you make a mistake, press the star key followed by the pound key. If you are ready to begin, press 9.

Enter your student ID number, followed by the pound key.

Now enter your personal identification number, followed by the pound key.

If you want to add a class, press 2, followed by the star key. Then press the class number, followed by the pound key.

Do you want to add another class? For "yes," press 9; for "no," press 6.

To review your schedule, press 5, followed by the pound key.

Introduction to Child Development, Psychology 321, Monday 7 to 10 p.m., James Hall, Room 222, Dr. Powers.

If you want to add another class, press 2. If you want to drop a class, press 3.

If you are ready to exit the registration system, press 9, followed by the pound key. Do not hang up the phone without pressing the pound key or your registration will not be recorded.

Thank you for using telephone registration.

UNIT 9
Keeping Up with the Times

Lesson 3, page 114

I'd like to make a toast to honor my dear friend, Rania. She has accepted challenges that have changed her life and have had a positive effect on the lives of others. She was able to deal with her fears of new technology at work. She learned a very difficult computerized sewing system. She learned it so well that she was promoted to manager of her department. We are here today to celebrate her success.

I remember when Rania first learned that her company was going to purchase computerized sewing machines. She said, "If I can't learn how to use the new machines, I'll get fired." She was so afraid that she would fail. She had worked on simple machines for so many years. Now, she loves the new machines.

Change is difficult for many of us. It can make us nervous and uncomfortable. It takes us away from what we know best. Yet, change brings opportunities for growth and for discovering new ways of doing things.

Rania is a perfect example of someone who accepted change by learning a new skill. That skill has opened new doors for her. Not only is she the manager, she is also thinking about starting her own business. She wants to make children's clothing and sell it on the Internet.

Rania, we really admire you. You have shown us that anything is possible if you put your mind to it. You've done a wonderful job, and I am proud to be your friend. Here's to your promotion and future business! Three cheers for Rania!

The US

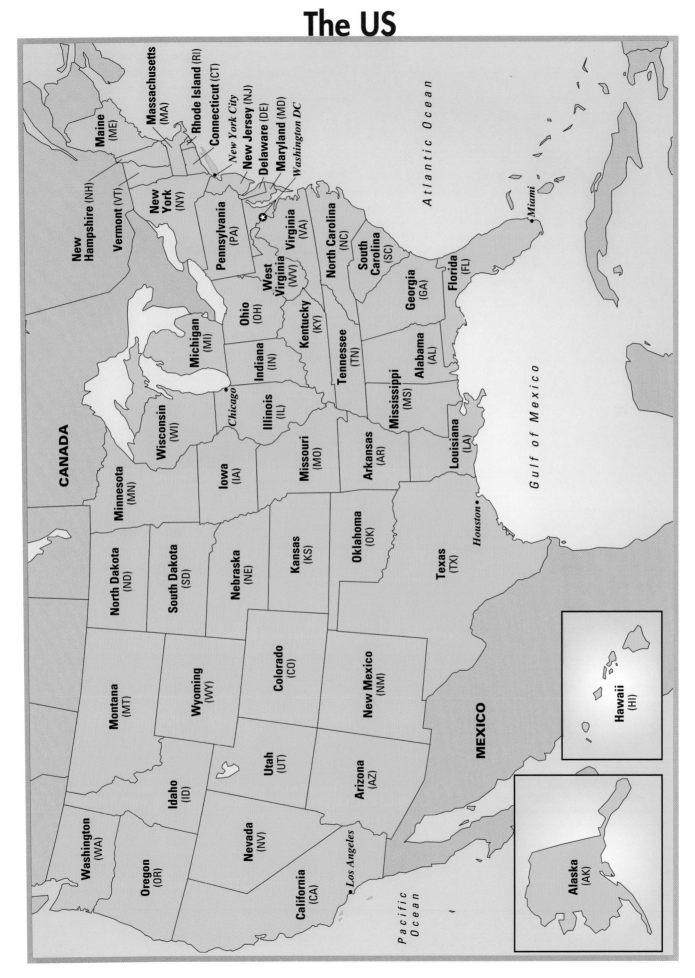

The World

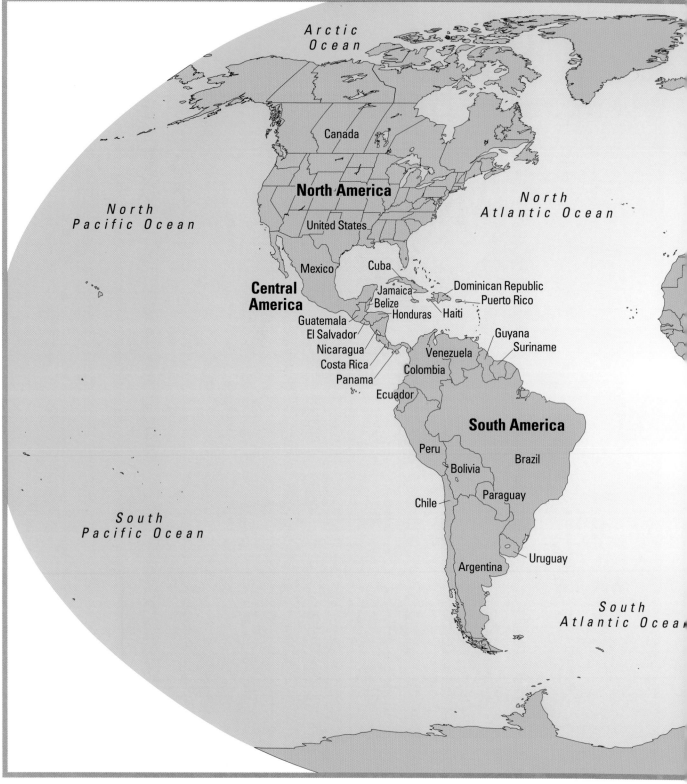

Arctic Ocean

Canada

North America

North Pacific Ocean

United States

North Atlantic Ocean

Mexico

Cuba

Central America

Jamaica

Dominican Republic

Belize

Puerto Rico

Guatemala

Honduras

Haiti

El Salvador

Nicaragua

Venezuela

Guyana

Suriname

Costa Rica

Colombia

Panama

Ecuador

South America

Peru

Brazil

Bolivia

South Pacific Ocean

Paraguay

Chile

Uruguay

Argentina

South Atlantic Ocean

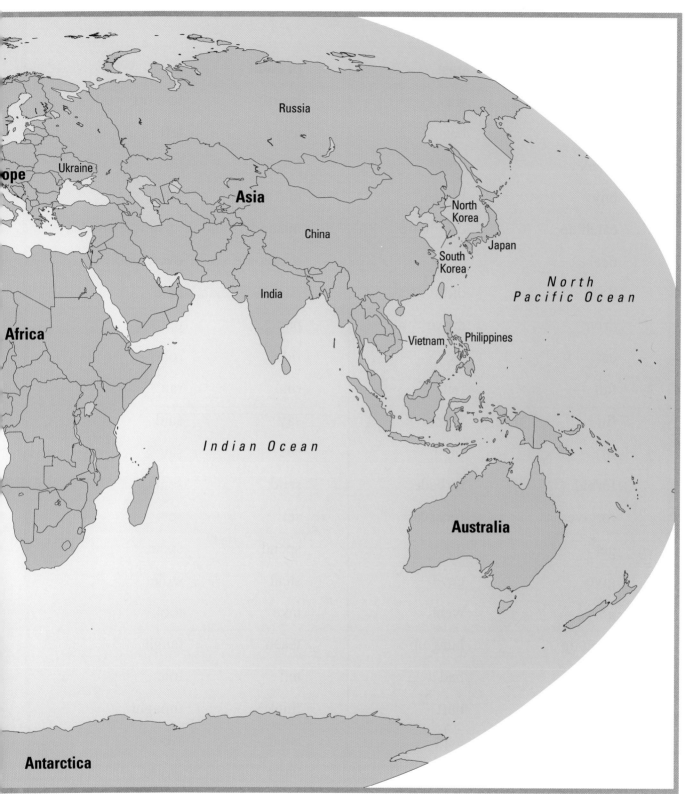

Russia

Ukraine

ope

Asia

China

India

North
Korea

Japan

South
Korea

North
Pacific Ocean

Africa

Vietnam   Philippines

Indian Ocean

Australia

Antarctica

Irregular Verbs

present	past	present	past
be	was	lay off	laid off
beat	beat	leave	left
break	broke	lose	lost
buy	bought	make	made
catch up	caught up	misunderstand	misunderstood
deal	dealt	overcome	overcame
do	did	pay	paid
drive	drove	put	put
eat	ate	ride	rode
fall	fell	run	ran
find	found	say	said
fit	fit	see	saw
forbid	forbade	send	sent
forgive	forgave	set	set
get	got	spend	spent
give	gave	steal	stole
go	went	take	took
hang up	hung up	teach	taught
have	had	tell	told
hurt	hurt	think	thought
keep	kept	wear	wore
know	knew	write	wrote

Writing Checklist and Metric Chart

❑ Did I take notes about my ideas before I started writing?

❑ Did I write a main idea at the beginning of the paragraph?

❑ Did I give details to explain my main idea?

❑ Do all my details relate to the main idea?

❑ Did I check my verbs for correct tense?

❑ Did I check for subject-verb agreement?

❑ Did I use complete sentences?

❑ Did I capitalize the first word of each sentence?

❑ Did I end every sentence with a period, question mark, or exclamation point?

❑ Did I check my spelling?

❑ Is my handwriting neat and easy to read?

METRIC CONVERSIONS

To Convert	To	Multiply by
LENGTH		
meters	feet	3.281
kilometers	miles	0.62
LIQUID		
liters	quarts	1.057
liters	gallons	.0264
WEIGHT		
grams	ounces	0.0353
kilograms	pounds	2.2046
TEMPERATURE		
Celsius	Fahrenheit	multiply by 1.8, then add 32

To Convert	To	Multiply by
LENGTH		
feet	meters	.03048
miles	kilometers	1.609
LIQUID		
quarts	liters	0.946
gallons	liters	3.785
WEIGHT		
ounces	grams	28.35
pounds	kilograms	0.4536
TEMPERATURE		
Fahrenheit	Celsius	subtract 32, then divide by 1.8

List of Grammar Terms

adjective – a word that describes a noun or a pronoun: *a **tall** tree, he is **handsome**.*

adverb – a word that tells more about a verb, adjective, or another adverb: *I **often** go shopping, a **very** tall tree, he talks **extremely** fast.*

article – a word used to mark a noun: *a boy, an apple, the cat.*

base form – the simplest form of a verb: *think, go, play.* Also called simple form.

clause – a group of words that contains a subject and a verb, and that forms part of a sentence: *Before I go to bed, I turn the heater off.*

comparative adjective – an adjective with *-er* on the end or *more* in front of it: *faster, more compact.*

compound sentence – a sentence consisting of two main clauses connected by *and, or,* or *but: June thinks that all babies are pretty, and so do I.*

direct speech – the use of somebody's exact words. In writing, quotation marks indicate direct speech: *He said, "I hate saying goodbye!"*

future – a verb tense that expresses expected action or a condition in the future. Formed by combining *will* or *be + going to* + simple form of the verb. ***I'll study** tomorrow. **I'm going to study** tomorrow.*

gerund – a verb used as a noun; formed by adding *-ing* to the simple form of the verb: *She's worried about **leaving** home.*

infinitive – a base verb form that is preceded by *to: I would like **to invite** him to my party.*

modal – a helping verb that adds to the meaning of a main verb: *can, could, may, must, have to, will, would. You **must** be on time.*

noncount noun – a noun that represents a group or type of item, such as *coffee, juice, fruit.* These nouns do not take plural forms. They are also called uncountable or mass nouns.

noun – a word used to name a person, place, thing, or idea. *My **brother** is from **Portland**. He values **honesty**.*

object – a noun, noun phrase, or noun clause that receives the action of a verb: *I hit **the ball**.*

past continuous/past progressive – a verb tense that expresses an action that began and ended in the past. It's often used with the simple past to show that something was happening at the time another action occurred. *She **was working** when she got the news.*

plural – a noun form that indicates more than one of a kind; formed by adding *-s, -es,* or *-ies* to the noun: *sweaters, boxes, babies.* Some nouns have irregular plurals: *men, women, children;* and some do not take plural forms: *money, heat, furniture.*

preposition – a word that shows the relationship between a noun and another part of a sentence: *in, on, under, over, around, about, with, for, to. I'm looking **for** a job.*

present continuous/present progressive – a verb tense that expresses an action that is happening at the present time. *Sierra **is sleeping** right now.*

present perfect – *have* or *has* with a past participle: refers to an action or situation that has a strong connection to the present. Often used with *for* and *since. Grace **has played** tennis for three years* (she still plays).

present perfect continuous – *have been* or *has been* with a present participle, used to refer to past events that continue in the present: *Rania **has been sewing** for many years.*

pronoun – a word that takes the place of a noun, such as *he, her, myself, it.* Most pronouns have different forms, depending on their use.

simple past – a verb tense that expresses a single, completed action or situation in the past. Formed by adding *-ed* to a regular verb, or by using the irregular past form. *Last night, we **saw** a full moon. We **stared** at it for a long time.*

simple present – a verb tense that expresses an action or situation that is habitual, is true now, or is always true. *She **smokes** a lot. I **go** to school. Glass **is** breakable.*

singular – a noun form that indicates one of a kind; *computer, week, school.*

subject – a noun, pronoun, noun phrase, or noun clause that performs an action expressed by the main verb. In English, the subject almost always comes near the beginning of a sentence. ***James** plays basketball. **He** is good.*

subject-verb agreement – necessity for verbs to agree with their subjects within a sentence. Normally, a singular or noncount noun takes a singular verb: *Margaret always walks to work; Brown rice is healthy.* A plural noun takes a plural verb: *My shoes are dirty.*

superlative adjective – an adjective with *-est* on the end or *most* in front of it: *easiest, most compact.*

verb – a word that expresses action or existence. *Samuel **takes** long naps; Madison **is** my niece.*

Topics

Grammar and Pronunciation